MAKING WORDS SING

What makes a classical song a song? In a wide-ranging discussion, covering such contrasting composers as Brahms and Berberian, Schubert and Kurtág, Jonathan Dunsby considers the nature of vocality in songs of the nineteenth and twentieth centuries. The essence and scope of poetic and literary meaning in the Lied tradition is subjected to close scrutiny against the backdrop of 'new musicological' thinking and music-theoretical orthodoxies. The reader is thus offered the best insights available within an evidence-based approach to musical discourse. Schoenberg figures conspicuously as both songsmith and theorist, and some easily comprehensible Schenkerian approaches are used to convey ideas of musical time and expressive focus. In this work of scholarship and theoretical depth, Professor Dunsby's highly original approach and engaging style will ensure its appeal to all practising musicians and students of Romantic and Modern music.

JONATHAN DUNSBY is Professor of Music at the University of Reading. He is the founding editor of the journal *Music Analysis*, and author of numerous articles on music of the past two centuries. His books include *Music Analysis in Theory and Practice*, co-authored with Arnold Whittall, and *Performing Music: Shared Concerns*.

Making Words Sing

Nineteenth- and Twentieth-Century Song

JONATHAN DUNSBY

CAMBRIDGE
UNIVERSITY PRESS

PUBLISHED BY THE PRESS SYNDICATE OF THE UNIVERSITY OF CAMBRIDGE
The Pitt Building, Trumpington Street, Cambridge, United Kingdom

CAMBRIDGE UNIVERSITY PRESS
The Edinburgh Building, Cambridge, CB2 2RU, UK
40 West 20th Street, New York, NY 10011–4211, USA
477 Williamstown Road, Port Melbourne, VIC 3207, Australia
Ruiz de Alarcón 13, 28014 Madrid, Spain
Dock House, The Waterfront, Cape Town 8001, South Africa

http://www.cambridge.org

© Jonathan Dunsby 2004

First published 2004

Printed in the United Kingdom at the University Press, Cambridge

Typeface Adobe Garamond 11/12.5 pt.   *System* LATEX 2ε   [TB]

A catalogue record for this book is available from the British Library

Library of Congress Cataloging-in-Publication Data
Dunsby, Jonathan.
Making words sing: nineteenth- and twentieth-century song / Jonathan Dunsby.
p.   cm.
Includes bibliographical references (p. 152) and index.
ISBN 0 521 83661 1
1. Songs – Analysis, appreciation.   2. Songs – 19th century – History and criticism.
3. Songs – 20th century – History and criticism.   I. Title.
MT120.D85   2004
782.42168 – dc22   2003065620

ISBN 0 521 83661 1 hardback

for B

Contents

Acknowledgements

In addition to more generations of undergraduate and graduate music students at the University of Reading than I care to count, other audiences have been subjected to parts of this book, to earlier versions of its ideas, to long or detailed analyses of which it contains samples and illustrations, and to the arguments that underpin it. These have included organizations to which I have been particularly grateful for significant opportunities for discussion and, it is hoped, improvement: the Caixa Foundation, Barcelona; the University of Cambridge; King's College, London; the Orpheus Institute, Ghent; the University of Oxford; Royal Holloway University of London; Trinity College, Dublin. I am grateful to the Arts and Humanities Research Board and to the University of Reading for funding research leave in 2000–1 without which this book would not have been possible. David Bretherton merits acknowledgement for his expert work in producing the music examples, but also my gratitude for his advice on a number of aspects of what the book says and how it says it, an influence of which I suspect he has not always been aware. And I thank Penny Souster of Cambridge University Press for her enduring confidence and gentle encouragement.

PERMISSIONS

Grateful thanks to:

Laaber-Verlag, Laaber, for kind permission to base part of Chapter 4 on my 'Friede auf Erden Op. 13', in *Arnold Schönberg: Interpretationen seiner Werke*, ed. Gerold Gruber, Laaber, Laaber-Verlag, 2002, 172–80.

Ashgate, Aldershot, for kind permission to base part of Chapter 4 on my 'All the Dancers know it and it is Valid for All Times: Goehr, Kafka and *The Law of the Quadrille*', in *Sing, Ariel: Essays and Thoughts for Alexander Goehr's Seventieth Birthday*, ed. Alison Latham, Aldershot, Ashgate, 2003, 171–9, and to reproduce the music examples.

Random House, New York, for kind permission to reproduce the translation on pp. 88–9 of Kafka's 'Before the Law', from *The Collected Short Stories of Franz Kafka*, ed. Nahum Glatzer, London, Penguin Books, 1988, 3–4.

Universal Edition, London, for kind permission to reproduce Exs 3.1 ('Seraphita') and 3.2–4 ('Vorgefühl') from Arnold Schoenberg, *Vier Lieder*, Op. 22, UE 6060; and Exs 4.7 and 4.8 from György Kurtág, *The Sayings of Péter Bornemisza*, Op. 7, UE 14493.

Peters Edition Limited, London, for kind permission to reproduce Exs 4.9 and 4.10 from Cathy Berberian, *Stripsody*, Edition Peters No. 66164.

Boosey and Hawkes Music Publishers Ltd, for kind permission to reproduce Exs 5.1 and 5.4–8 from Aaron Copland, *12 Songs of Emily Dickinson*, 'Going to Heaven!', B&H 17865.

Introduction

The literature on words and music is vast. This was already the case even before the proliferation of writing about Western classical music that was evident in books, journals, encyclopaedias, and more ephemeral sources during the 1980s and 1990s, not only in English, and not only restricted to 'pure' studies but also in the realm of intra- and intercultural research. So why is yet another book needed? If it is difficult to pinpoint a conclusive answer to that question, the direction of thought leading to *Making Words Sing* is clear enough.

Firstly, musicological thinking moves on from one short period to the next as each new wave of writers brings fresh insight and knowledge, and in particular as taste changes. For example, in the specialized field of music analysis – on which I draw throughout these pages intermittently, although without importing too much of its fascinating and necessary jargon and technical routines, or, all being well, its tendency to redescribe the known and even to state the obvious – a sense of the appropriate repertoire has changed beyond recognition in recent years. There was a time, say twenty years ago, when those interested directly or vicariously in music theory and analysis would rightly joke that 'analysis' could be defined roughly as: the detailed study of the music of Anton Webern. And if that pleasantry is nowadays wearing very thin, this is a sign of the broadening of technical engagement with music that some would say has led to dilution and lack of focus, but that others welcome as a way forward from the perceived tyrannies of high modernism in its ascetic intellectualism, and of structuralism in its obsession with the apparent mechanisms of art. At least it is no surprise now if the repertoire drawn on in a book is not either 'Romantic' or 'Modern' but both, reflecting this author's conviction that composers of the twentieth century were always much closer to their predecessors than historians, by and large, were able to understand and convey effectively; and perhaps even more intriguingly that composers of the nineteenth century were often far in 'advance' of historical interpretation, and their work could remain so, long after their deaths. Think only, for example, of the complete transformation of musical form ('form' as understood from the model to be found in Beethoven) worked out by Schubert over hundreds of musical compositions during Beethoven's lifetime and in the further, golden months until Schubert's death in 1828, only to be misunderstood by about five generations of musicologists in any number of languages, infatuated (who can blame them?) with Beethoven's way of writing music.

Secondly, there emerged in musicology of the 1980s and 1990s not only a rather priggish liberalism coupled with a naïve – in my view – psychologism that masqueraded as a kind of psychoanalytical savvy without, if the truth be told, having much at all to do with psychotherapeutic scholarship or understanding, but also much more positively, what has been called a 'eucrasia', a sort of general wellbeing based on openness, in technical musical discourse. To some extent this has to be put down to a growing discomfort among those who write about music with 'formalism' in any of its many guises, including the 'classic' music-analytical approaches enshrined in various textbooks of that subdiscipline.[1] It was not so much that 'meaning' was somehow rediscovered in the critical free-for-all that often seemed to be sanctioned by 'New Musicology', but that histories – the use of reliable historical data at least – could once again be part of the *interpretation* of the past rather than the past being merely, purely, supposedly, revisited.

Thirdly, and possibly most importantly at least as to intellectual matters, the eucrasia that relied on the readmission of historical fact (albeit symbolic fact) on to the critical palette brought with it the possibility of what I call an 'evidence-based' musical discourse that seems able to mediate between extremes of structuralism on the one hand and critical fantasy on the other. This epistemological position has long been championed, and argued out in detail, by Jean-Jacques Nattiez in the area of music semiotics.[2] One may well ask why, then, *Making Words Sing* is not based on Nattiez's subtle methodology and its careful terminology. Actually, in many respects it is, covertly perhaps, in that I have always tried to keep clearly in mind the three 'poles' of the 'tripartition' that invites us to be clear at all times about whether we are discussing matters of production, reception

---

[1] Perhaps the most widely used analytical textbook has been Nicholas Cook's *A Guide to Musical Analysis*, London, Dent, 1987.

[2] Among his voluminous writings I particularly recommend, as to applied methodology, *Wagner Androgyne: A Study in Interpretation*, Princeton, Princeton University Press, 1993, and for the broad sweep of his thinking, *The Battle of Chronos and Orpheus*, Oxford, Oxford University Press, 2004; this in addition to his standard work to date in English, *Music and Discourse: Toward a Semiology of Music*, Princeton, Princeton University Press, 1990.

or description/explanation ('poiesis', 'esthesis' or the 'neutral' level), and nearly always to keep in mind that there will be some specific interaction among these poles;[3] and I have always tried to keep in mind the kinds of meaning that are supposed to be on offer in any musical explanation or musicohistorical argument. Yet a building ought to stand up once the scaffolding is removed, and without the smell of wet cement lingering; one wants to see the marionette dance without also seeing the strings. Nothing, however, is deliberately *hidden* in my work here. Where epistemology and methodology are implicit rather than discussed in detail (and implicitness is not uncommon in the pages to follow), this is for the reader's benefit, it is hoped, and it is of course at the author's own risk. A similar risk is taken on those occasions where I do feel it necessary to comment on issues of knowledge and approach, and to the extent that this narrative does tend to carry along its own critique – often saying or trying to say *why* it is saying what it is saying – then the reader can be assured of one simple motivation in the author: enthusiasm.

Finally by way of general introduction, however, and although this, too, may be an 'intellectual' matter, there is what has the guise of a more overtly musical question, which is why one would want to be so concerned with words, with song, with text, with 'vocality'. I touch on this in different terms in Chapter 1 below, but in this less formal introductory setting I simply say that 'song' is what music is all about: a radically indefensible statement, of course, once we begin to unpick it historically, aesthetically, philosophically, yet it is also a kind of truism for anyone acculturalized to modern Western music – in other words, for the modern 'music lover', or Donald Tovey's 'ordinary listener' of yore (see p. 69), or Mozart's 'amateurs' as well as 'cognoscenti' of centuries gone by. This is not only a physiological matter, an assertion of the primacy or certainly of the 'firstness' of the voice in human development both of the species and of the individual. In our contemporary minds, too, words and, in the case of most people, music of one kind or another intermingle, almost whether we like it or not. Although this phenomenon has been as little studied in the pure or the human sciences according to their own agendas as it has been in the 'humanities' with any serious grasp of scientific 'reality', everyone knows that as a fact of human experience this is true. Often music and words are understood to be in apposition with, even opposition to, each other, and for specialist enquiries

---

[3] I attempted to formulate the essence of Nattiez's approach, at least in respect of music-analytical procedures, in 'Thematic and Motivic Analysis', in *The Cambridge History of Western Music Theory*, ed. Thomas Christensen, Cambridge, Cambridge University Press, 2002, 907–26.

this can be an important distinction.[4] Eventually, however, there must be a place for taking things together, as the 'vast'-ness of the literature referred to above seems to indicate.

More specifically, it will be apparent that whereas in these discussions of ideas and propositions the ideas and propositions are fully present and where appropriate discussed in considerable depth, their whole object, on the other hand, the repertoire of beautiful music (and if it is not always pretty music, then it is certainly always memorable), is missing at least in the sense that it is not literally to be 'heard' or directly experienced in a book. This is a familiar brute fact of books about music. Perhaps it has a special piquancy in a context where the music itself already has a profoundly inveigling reality as it draws on our linguistic and musical attention at the same time. How so?, as anyone would be likely to ask, is one way of asking what this book is about. Music and words, words with music, surely amount to a special kind of musical experience, although we might speculate, and learn from the prehistory of human kind, that it is also the most natural kind of musical experience in its plenitude of engagement of human faculties. And because it is a special and by definition multifaceted experience, then it needs to be experienced unmediated, if any music does (as of course all music does at some level). All the music mentioned here is readily available in recordings, and its scores are readily available from libraries or from their publishers. In one case at least, Copland's Emily Dickinson songs, even images of the composer's sketches are readily available, online at the flick of an electronic switch, and a good deal of other virtual information relevant to the music, composers, poets, critics and other characters and topics of this text exists on the worldwide web, although I decided not to point to any of it or render any of it integral to reading and absorbing the book.

I have indicated in essence what this book is about by mentioning the 'special piquancy' of vocal music. I am in search here of an understanding of what is going to be called 'vocality'. Now clearly there is the potential to irritate the reader in using a rather effete word such as vocality. It has a specific (and, here, irrelevant) technical meaning in linguistics by referring to the quality of a sound that is voiced (as with the sound usually denoted by the letter 'd' in English rather than the unvoiced 't') or to the nature of a sound as being a vowel. I am interested rather in its meaning as, according to the *Oxford English Dictionary*, 'the quality of having voice' and more particularly 'vocal quality or nature'; but of course in that I am referring by

---

[4] Hans Keller offered notably trenchant accounts of this dissociation; see, for example, his *Criticism*, London, Faber, 1987.

'vocal' not in the primary sense to what is spoken or oral, but to the musical meaning of the word, 'performed by or composed for the voice'. Rather in the way that the great Romanian ethnomusicologist Constantin Brăiloiu asked us to consider seriously in what respect any music can be said to have been 'composed' by one person,[5] which may *appear* to be the case here and there in world cultures and histories (songs 'by' Schubert or Copland, say, as we assert unquestioningly in Chapter 5, while straining to capture what is unique about them, and unthinkable though these songs would be without their cultural histories, the 'style' that makes them comprehensible at all), so I want to ask here in what respect some music can be said to express vocality, other than in the trite fact of it being music in which words are sung. Vocality certainly overlaps with concepts to be found in two centuries' worth and more of discussion of vocal music, but I do not think everything has been said that can be said. Vocality as exposed here might be thought, for example, to be more or less coextensive with Lawrence Kramer's notion of 'songfulness', but this is not so. 'Songfulness', Kramer insists, 'is a fusion of vocal and musical utterance judged to be both pleasurable and suitable independent of verbal content. It is the positive quality of singing-in-itself: just singing.' Add to this his idea of 'loss of meaning', that 'songfulness makes meaning extraneous, if not downright superfluous', and the long and the short of Kramer's position has been aired.[6] It makes some kind of informal sense, undoubtedly, when we think of ourselves as being 'lost' in performing or listening to song, and it almost goes without saying that whatever verbal language and musical language are in themselves, they are not a mere addition of the two intact 'languages' when they occur together. But as I understand Kramer (from study of as many of his writings on music as have been available to me, which is probably most of them), he is for all the elaborate enjoyment to be gained from his critical perceptions merely reducing 'song' to some kind of idealized third language that is beyond analysis, beyond interpretation. Not the least of my objections to this position is its unhelpful implication that somehow we do have a clear picture of what 'musical language' is itself prior to the 'fusion' of which Kramer writes, and in different ways writes very often. We do not, as the philosopher Peter Kivy has tried to argue (see Chapter 1, pp. 14–15), in my

---

[5] Constantin Brăiloiu, 'Reflections on Collective Musical Creation', in *Problems of Ethnomusicology*, Cambridge, Cambridge University Press, 1984, 102–9.

[6] Lawrence Kramer, 'Beyond Words and Music: An Essay on Songfulness', in *Musical Meaning: Toward a Critical History*, Berkeley, University of California Press, 2002, 51–67; 53 and 63 respectively. Kramer has written extensively and stimulatingly on words and music, and some of his other ideas are quoted or discussed further in these pages.

view rather successfully and certainly persuasively. On the contrary, our ability to get at any of the essentials of vocality will rest crucially on the depth and substance of our music-analytical hermeneutics in the first place. There can be no other worthwhile starting point, or so I shall try to argue and exemplify.

* * *

Although I am not offering a theory of vocality or anything approaching it, we shall nevertheless have to explore notions of music and text as interacting entities, which I aim to do in Chapter 1, focusing in the second section on poetry and language, and in the third on 'untheory', which is my word here to capture the sense I seek to share with the reader in which a 'theory' of music and words is not something easily imagined or obviously desirable: this is no eccentric position to take, in that Schoenberg seems to have thought so, too, as will be described and discussed; and what Schoenberg thought is worth any of us thinking about. In Chapter 2 there is a complete 'reading' of Brahms's song 'Von ewiger Liebe', 'complete' in the most modest sense that I discuss all of the song, 'reading' in the equally modest attempt to indicate one pathway – a hermeneutical pathway, I believe it would be right to call it – through music that can be understood in as many different ways (musicians like to say, in theatrically exaggerated expression of their theoretical inefficacy) as there are listeners. Actually, there is just the *one* way to hear this song, if you subscribe to the astonishingly powerful explanatory theory of tonal masterpieces elaborated by Heinrich Schenker and filled out, supplemented, some would say enriched, by at least three generations of Schenkerian practitioners since the 1930s. There is no doubt that Schenker was some kind of musical Freud taking us deep into stories of the musical mind, or, as he would have written, the mind of the musical 'genius'. Like it or not, Schenkerian theory is integral to understanding – to being able to keep up with – one important strand of musical thought in the twentieth century; I, who used to ask why Schenker could be expected still to stalk twentieth-first-century musicology,[7] must be the first to admit it.

Chapter 3, for those made to squirm at all by formalist, explanatory theory (although I hope to have made Chapter 2 as comfortable as possible, perhaps even enjoyable), takes a nonprescriptive view of a song by Schoenberg, 'Premonition', Op. 22, No. 4, music that is in contrast modernistic for its times – it is, for instance, 'atonal' – and raises rather different

---

[7] See my 'Recent Schenker: The Poetic Power of Intelligent Calculation (or, The Emperor's Second Set of New Clothes)', in *Music Analysis*, 18/2, July 1999, 263–73; 263.

questions about vocality. I have deliberately chosen here music that is 'hard to understand', not merely in my opinion, but taking my lead from Alban Berg's essay on the early music of his revered teacher. Is vocality something of a different order in this context? We shall discover that it is probably not, but the context leads to many different kinds of investigation that would hardly arise in Brahms or in Classical and Romantic music, and that begin to consolidate here the potential range and depth of the subject even within the narrow constraints of a repertoire and an approach in this book that have been necessarily imposed on a project designed to be concentrated and digestible, and anything but comprehensive. If Chapter 4 hardly goes on to open Pandora's Box, since again the view of time and place is not allowed to waver too much, nevertheless it offers a potpourri from the sacred to the profane, from the European to the American, from notes to gurgles, and its actors – Schoenberg once more, Goehr, Kurtág (with Schumann), Berberian – would not be too puzzled to find themselves in each other's company, every one a dogged seeker of vocality, and in Berberian's case a world-class practitioner of it. Here we also expand on some of the generalized discussion of poetry and language from Chapter 1, since each text – late Romantic religious, early existentialist, medieval eschatological, post-World-War-Two comic strip – steps aside from the mainstream of the poetic lyric that can be read about (and should be) in any number of studies of the Lied, chanson, art-song and the like. Chapter 5 then offers some final relaxation, its own kind of musical eucrasia as (in chronological order of birth) Goethe, Schubert, Dickinson and Copland are knitted into a picture of vocality in examples where it is at its most sublime, it can surely be agreed, and looking out across the nineteenth and twentieth centuries as over the same waters, when love and death were constants, as always. This will have been, it will be clear, a very particular kind of journey, not a 'history', not a theory, but an exploration. It aims to be coherent but it is also recognized that the limits it sets itself are pragmatic rather than epistemological; these limits have not been inevitable, and if some use can be made by some readers of these pages it will undoubtedly be as much or more through what they suggest as through what they determine.

* * *

Too much introspection is perhaps some kind of neurosis and always in danger of stemming creative processes, including those of the reader, but a few words about the apparent origins of this study may provide some useful orientation here. In some convoluted way it seems that the book title was, on this occasion at least, a genuine impetus to its completion, for it was a surprisingly clear guide, elliptical though it may be, as to inclusion and exclusion, as to tone, as to where to begin each level of enquiry and also a guide as to where to stop it. Who, it was being asked above via Brăiloiu (see p. 5), can ever accurately be said to be the 'author' of a piece of music? Similarly, it is not at all clear now, and it matters even less, just where the title *Making Words Sing* came from, and if there is some person or some previous publication or constellation of words to which acknowledgement deserves to be made but now through the mists of time cannot be made, no offence is intended. Without doubt, though, a primary impetus in general came from the author's formative experience of being given a project to do in a very much younger incarnation: the suggestion was to compare settings of Goethe's 'Mignon' poem 'Kennst du das Land?' by Beethoven, Schubert and Schumann, while little knowing at the time that there were many dozens of settings in the nineteenth and twentieth centuries, that only a few years previously an entire graduate thesis had been devoted to a comparative study of some of the most interesting settings,[8] or that one day an entire large file of my own subsequent studies of 'Kennst du das Land?' was going to be excluded from *Making Words Sing* (despite the original intention to include it) because this is not, in the end, a philological book, one that can comfortably carry a basically comparative exercise.

The revelation, however, was quite specific. Through it one could experience for the first time that a setting of a text is unique, that the creative urge in a composer of what some call 'genius' can transcend what the literary critic Harold Bloom was to name the 'anxiety of influence', that the self-same words can be made to sing in different ways.[9] How? Again it was only much later that I came to see this as a specific instance of a general class of questions, not least when one considers the rather obvious fact that certain texts have been made to sing not across the decades but across the millennia – especially perhaps the Mass, as Georgiades discussed with such musicological virtuosity.[10] And needless to say malleability was not only a phenomenon of sacred music, as the history of opera as well as music drama amply demonstrates: one need only ponder the fact that, as Jean-Jacques Nattiez notes in a study of Baudelaire's Wagner-reception, 'in actual fact,

[8] Donald Ivey, 'The Romantic Synthesis in Selected Settings of Goethe's "Kennst du das Land?"', DMA dissertation, University of Illinois at Urbana-Champaign, 1962.

[9] Harold Bloom's book *The Anxiety of Influence: A Theory of Poetry*, New York, Oxford University Press, 1973, became fashionable in certain quarters of American music theory in the 1980s and 1990s, although it never became clear what it adds to our understanding of musical influences. Its undoubted strength lay in the refinement it brought to the notions of literary influence, above all in poetry, and it is easy to see that the more specific and useful it was in poetics, the less applicable to musical epistemology it was likely to be.

[10] Thrasybulos Georgiades, *Music and Language: The Rise of Western Music as Exemplified in Settings of the Mass*, Cambridge, Cambridge University Press, 1982.

Wagner never stopped revising *Tannhäuser* over thirty years, every time the opera was given a new performance', and Nattiez tellingly subtitles the closing section of his study of *Tannhäuser* 'A Work that is Complete but Unfinished'.[11] An endless deferral of 'meaning' in music with words of which *Tannhäuser* is one of a number of spectacular, well-known examples goes a long way to explaining how certain words may be enshrined in starkly distinct musical manifestations, and it is part of the potential continuum of that thought to ask, then, what in any particular manifestation makes it what it is. The elusive intermingling of the fluidity of meaning on the one hand, and the stark specificity of works of art on the other – that specificity that is, for instance, what I understood in general by the philosopher Theodor Adorno's many references to the 'truth content' of a piece of music – is what I mean by 'making' words to 'sing'.

[11] Nattiez, *The Battle of Chronos and Orpheus*.

CHAPTER I

An introduction with no words, with intended words, and untheory

MUSIC WITHOUT WORDS

One of the most clearly descriptive generic titles of Western music of recent centuries is also one of the most intriguing: 'Das Lied ohne Worte', the Song without Words. Mendelssohn published six volumes of forty-eight such pieces in 1832–45, often charming, sometimes deeply moving, in some cases composed simply, very 'playable' and in 'folk' style, in other cases – rather less commonly – extremely skilful compositionally in ways that are easy to perceive (for example, in the A-flat 'Duetto', No. 18, which combines on one instrument the female and male 'voice', separately as well as 'singing' together, with full piano accompaniment).[1] The very title 'Song without Words' triggers unusual questions. Why, for instance, would anyone *want* to write a wordless song? How do we know in the absence of words that a 'song' is what this kind of music is designed to be? And is music of this kind supposed to be *instead* of song, some kind of complement to the 'real' thing, or is it perhaps the best that can be done alone at the piano (assuming that the pianist lacks the ability to sing and play simultaneously to the same standard?), and is it thus a makeshift of some sort?[2]

Julian Rushton is right, I believe, to point in his essay 'Music and the Poetic' to the aura of heightened expression and what will be called here a

---

[1] The standard work on this repertoire is Christa Jost, *Mendelssohns Lieder ohne Worte*, Tützing, Schneider, 1988.

[2] In *Schumann's Dichterliebe and Early Romantic Poetics: Fragmentation of Desire*, Cambridge, Cambridge University Press, 2002, 57, Beate Perrey reminds us that there were at least two such genres, Schumann having written about those Songs without Words 'inspired by poems' (he is thinking of the composer Taubert) compared with Mendelssohn's, which, as Schumann wrote, 'perhaps stimulate one to poeticize'. A balance between the more literal and the more suggestive was already well in place in the early nineteenth century when Beethoven famously mentioned that his Pastoral Symphony was less concerned with depiction than with feelings. Whether or not it is true that Mendelssohn's sister Fanny Hensel actually invented the title *Lied ohne Worte*, it is certainly the case that this genre was strongly connected with the feminine world of domestic musicmaking.

kind of 'transvocality' in this period, which makes the Song without Words seem a most natural genre in the wider context:

An absence of specificity is a vital part of the Romantic project which finds poetry in unmediated sound . . . The listener experiences a song in an unknown language; either music has thrown off the yoke of poetry, while retaining the musical forms to which poetry gave rise, or the penetration of music by poetry has reached a point where, saturated by poetic essence, music would be hampered by the precision of verbal imagery.[3]

Not only in Mendelssohn, but from Tomášek's piano pieces of 1807 all the way through to Mahler's 'Adagietto' (from the Fifth Symphony of 1904) this urge towards transvocality led composers to sustain the potential hegemony of nonvocal music that historians from then until now have seen as being initially consolidated by Beethoven (for a brief comment on Schumann's take on this in his songs, at least as Kramer formulates it, see p. 97). Among the leading thinkers who celebrated this Romantic urge, few can have been more trenchant than Friedrich Nietzsche, writing 'On Music and Words' in about 1871:

Imagine, after all preconditions, what an undertaking it must be to write music for a poem, that is, to wish to illustrate a poem by means of music, in order to secure a conceptual language for music in this way. What an inverted world! An undertaking that strikes one as if a son desired to beget his father! Music can generate images that will always be mere schemata, as it were examples of its real universal content. But how should the image, the representation, be capable of generating music? Not to speak of the notion that the concept or, as has been said, the 'poetical idea' should be capable of doing this! While it is certain that a bridge leads from the mysterious castle of the musician into the free country of images – and the lyric poet walks across it – it is impossible to proceed in the opposite direction, although there are said to be some people who have the delusion that they have done this.[4]

Nietzsche's essay was designed in part, it is believed, to follow up Eduard Hanslick's pioneering 1854 thoughts *On The Musically Beautiful*[5] but without the corollary in Hanslick of an attachment to the 'aesthetic' in musical meaning. On the contrary, says Nietzsche, the 'emotions' cannot ever 'show' the 'sanctuary of music', but only 'symbolize' it. The potential hegemony of transvocality – 'potential' in that actually 'making words sing' did

---

[3] Julian Rushton, 'Music and the Poetic', in *The Cambridge History of Nineteenth-Century Music*, ed. Jim Samson, Cambridge, Cambridge University Press, 2002, 165–6.

[4] See Carl Dahlhaus, *Between Romanticism and Modernism*, Berkeley, University of California Press, 1980, Appendix, 106–19; 109.

[5] Indianapolis, Hackett Publishing Company, 1986.

after all remain a central drive of the Romantic and Modern centuries –
never changed essentially in the post-Romantic period: in the 'typical' composer's oeuvre of the late twentieth century, that of Carter, say, or Boulez,
or Takemitsu, we see the familiar menu of the vocal and the 'instrumental',
looking pretty much like typical composers' worklists of one or two hundred
years earlier.

Transvocality as a bald historical fact brought in its wake some deep issues
that it will not be our business here to investigate, although they surely need
to be noted as a foil to the narratives to come. First, for example, the very
performance of song and other forms of vocal/instrumental music (starting,
as it were, with the choral finale of Beethoven's Ninth Symphony) had a
sort of persistent, voiceless 'double' in domestic and public musicmaking.
This interplay is very familiar to many modern music lovers through traditional jazz, the vast majority of whose exponents are long deceased (its
first 'rage' having been, as Glenn Watkins notes, as long ago as 1909–14)[6]
but still a presence in our culture through sound and visual recordings,
and living on stylistically in many facets of popular music: most of us
will be aware that one of the epitomes of 'great' jazz improvisation was
to attempt to imitate the flexible pitch and timbre of the human voice,
especially by those instruments where this can work well (trumpet and
saxophone in particular); indeed, part of the enthralling cultural richness
in such a great singer as Ella Fitzgerald was the looping back of instrumental effects into the toolkit of her consummate vocal technique that was
in turn a model, an ideal, to which jazz instrumentalists from 52nd Street
to jazz's remotest outposts would try to measure up in nuance and virtuosity. Yet the interplay between voice and its simulacrums and rivals goes
back a long way in the history of virtuosity; it is precisely the site, nearly
two centuries ago, in which the contemporary historian Kramer places the
emblematic Liszt and the whole class of voiceless Romantic heroes on violin
(Paganini, of course) and, more prolifically, on piano – including women
'maestros':

The virtuoso is riddled with ambivalence. He can be identified equally well with
the extremes of transcendental expressiveness and cheap, flashy display. Unlike the
singer, he cannot choose between modesty and show (the key aesthetic issue in
Liszt's day and earlier); he cannot, so to speak, be either Orpheus or a siren, but
must always be both. *Unlike the singer, whose instrument is invisible, the virtuoso must
show what he does* and thus so court the charge that showing is all he does. He thus

[6] Glenn Watkins, *Pyramids at the Louvre: Music, Culture, and Collage from Stravinsky to the Postmodernists*, Cambridge, Mass., Harvard University Press, 1994, 4.

becomes a magnet for the multiple ambivalences that have haunted the concept of appearance itself at least since Plato – in relation to the body, theatricality, deception, rhetoric, and the like.[7]

Note how Kramer presents this transvocal phenomenon as a sort of permanent crisis in Western culture identified as long ago as Plato, the Plato of philosophy rather than cultural theory.

It is, in other words, a crisis that goes deeper than the merely sociological, which brings us to the second, even more complex issue that we can only hope, here, to take in our stride without seeking to plumb its depths or, least of all, begin to think of resolving it. For vocality, transvocality and nonvocality are a fact of cultural life and of physiological as well as epistemological life: just as – or better, in rather the same way that – we have hands, we have manufactured tools that perform functions that we can think of as 'handlike' even though they go far beyond our actual physical ability, and we have machines that completely transcend the human (think only, for example, of machines that move on wheels); so we have knowledge within our own experience, while also being aware of and continually making use of knowledge that seems almost boundless and that lies permanently beyond the person, in that we cannot imagine a single human being who would know, say, a small fraction of what is contained in a small library. Whether or not such illustrations of human dichotomy between the 'person' and the 'world' are more or less accurate than is needed, are better at elucidating or in danger of confusing, whether they are strong images or just too vague truly to capture the sense of rift in human thought and action, all the same the philosophical stakes are high and are certainly dramatized in the field of music.

This is hardly a modern phenomenon. Like Peter Kivy below, Daniel Chua in his essay 'Vincenzo Galilei, Modernity and the Division of Nature' traces it to around four hundred years ago and claims that its effects were to be found throughout the worlds of Classical and Romantic music: 'Music is set in opposition to itself as subject and object; human values are set against scientific facts, vocal melody against instrumental harmony, opera against the symphony. It is this division that defines the quarrel between Rousseau and Rameau in the eighteenth century and the debate between Wagner and Hanslick in the nineteenth.' True, in general. But it is unsettling when Chua shows his epistemological hand more clearly: 'What happens to music when the world is unsung? It becomes instrumental. In opposition to the

---

[7] Lawrence Kramer, *Musical Meaning: Toward a Critical History*, Berkeley, University of California Press, 2002, 69 (my emphasis).

pastoral, instrumental music is an *empty* sign, lacking the *magical* presence that only the voice can re-present.'[8] For a scholarly text there is a high degree of emphasis – hyperbole almost if one were to be supercritical of the text itself, passion if one were to speculate on the attitude of the writer at this point – in those words 'empty' and 'magical'. If instrumental music is an 'empty' sign, in the sense that one can easily agree, the sense of it not carrying verbal semantic associations, that does not seem to lead logically to a contrast with some 'magical' presence (rather than, say, some more neutral concept such as the 'vocally semantic'?). Not that Chua is necessarily wrong in the least, but note the leap he has made to not a logical contrast (to everyday semantic vocality) but a mystical enshrinement of a hallowed opposite (the 'magical' presence of the voice); and in truth one imagines that he would be in awe of this presence even if it were to be shorn of its very last vestiges of the semantic.[9] What Chua finds in music considered from this point of view, it seems to me, is something categorical, symbolic, totemic, almost language-defying. I shall return to one good word for its most haunting quality: 'otherness'.

Kivy, meanwhile, believes that if – and here he seems to be in complete agreement with Chua – this is no purely modern phenomenon, it does remain an urgent contemporary issue and is perhaps more problematic than Chua is able to convey. We are at only the early stages of confronting it, Kivy wants to remind us:

Since the end of the sixteenth century there have been *two* arts of music: the fine art of musical text setting, which is basically the art of representing human expression in musical tones, and the decorative art of absolute music. Recognizing this simple fact frees us from the impossible philosophical task of finding a theory or some other kind of conceptual analysis that can enable us to understand absolute music as one of the fine arts. In a word, it *isn't* . . . The recognition of absolute music as a decorative rather than a fine art opens up to us a host of new and, to me, both exciting and important problems that may have implications quite beyond the confines of musical aesthetics . . . We have paid little attention to the decorative arts in our philosophies, tend to disvalue them in comparison to the arts of content, and are, at present, ill equipped to talk about them.[10]

---

[8] Daniel Chua, 'Vincenzo Galiler, Modernity and the Division of Nature', in *Music Theory and Natural Order from the Renaissance to the Early Twentieth Century*, ed. Suzannah Clark and Alexander Rehding, Cambridge, Cambridge University Press, 2001, 17–29; 19 and 27 (my emphasis) respectively.

[9] How possible this abstract vocality might be is a matter for speculation. I leave the reader to ponder whether such high-art '*vocalises*' as, say, those exquisite examples by Rachmaninov and Villa-Lobos, or the anything but unsophisticated, if nevertheless earthy, Inuit throat games, all the way to any casual human humming one might hear, are truly asemantic.

[10] Peter Kivy, *The Fine Art of Repetition: Essays in the Philosophy of Music*, Cambridge, Cambridge University Press, 1993, 371–3.

The transvocal, that is, has barely been theorized adequately. It is not something we are yet in a position to say we understand in any really useful way. All I would add in this context is that Kivy need not be quite so optimistic about the 'fine art' either, since how words are made to sing still bears a great deal of investigation. In carrying out such investigation, one must keep a wary eye out for topics in 'absolute' music appearing inside a Trojan horse, ready to subvert the music-and-text agenda because they are themselves such fascinating issues. This last is clearly one strand that Joseph Kerman had in mind in his provocative and deliciously entitled essay 'How We Got into Analysis, and How to Get Out',[11] accusing music analysts not only of having become myopically obsessed with 'organicism' in the canonical Western repertoire, but also with failing to see what the music is crucially about, at least when it comes to vocal music and their allegedly habitual downplaying of textual 'meaning'. How effectively one can subvert the potential lures of transvocal critical ideology remains to be seen and will be for the reader to judge.

'WHERE CAN WE LIVE BUT DAYS?'

'What are days for?', asked Philip Larkin in the first line of his poem 'Days' of 1953; and then he gave us his short answer, that 'Days are where we live'.[12] Larkin's strategy here – if strategy is the right word for a poet who is so playful in general with our expectations as readers – is to make us think about a question that we have possibly, probably, never asked ourselves before, because it simply did not occur to us in quite that way. We take 'days' so much for granted, I would guess, that it would be quite understandable if someone's response to Larkin's question were to ask in return, 'What does he mean, "*for*"?' Understandable, yet unlikely, since anyone who sits down to read a poem, or who hears a poem somehow and knows that that is what it is, is expecting the unexpected. If the poem were to begin, more simply, 'How long are days?', for example, we would hardly be expecting line 2 to state the blindingly obvious, 'twenty-four hours', and if it did our expectation of the unexpected would only increase, waiting for line 3 and beyond to tell us something – 'Each hour can last/ a lifetime' perhaps, or maybe 'In the Arctic, half a kilometre/ If you're lucky'.

---

[11] Joseph Kerman, 'How We Got into Analysis, and How to Get Out', in *Critical Inquiry*, 7, 1980, 311–31. The discussion was elaborated in Kerman's *Musicology*, London, Fontana, 1985, especially in the chapter 'Analysis, Theory, and New Music', 60–112.
[12] *Philip Larkin: Collected Poems*, ed. Anthony Thwaite, London, Faber, 1988, 67.

The musical parallels with 'expecting the unexpected' in poetic language are fairly obvious and have often been discussed in the musicological literature. Indeed, such parallels were theorized long ago by Leonard Meyer, who distinguished neatly between 'recurrence', which creates 'closure and a feeling of completeness', and 'reiteration', which does lead to our expecting the unexpected: 'Reiteration does not necessarily give rise to expectations of further repetition. On the contrary, if repetition is fairly exact and persistent, change rather than further repetition is expected, i.e., saturation sets in.'[13] Think of almost any conventional nursery-rhyme tune or, say, a folksong, and this musical interplay of reiteration generating change, and recurrence generating closure, is likely to be obvious – 'Three Blind Mice', for instance, 'Frère Jacques', and many more probably known to any reader. At around the time in the middle of the last century that Meyer was taking a behaviourist, information-theory approach to ideas of reiteration and recurrence in modern (if not contemporaneous) Western music, Schoenberg was teaching these matters more technically, distinguishing in thematic theory between the musical 'period', which begins with contrasting ideas and thus tends to continue with recurrence, and the musical 'sentence', which begins with repetition or varied repetition and therefore tends to continue by way of contrast, prior to recurrence.[14] There are, of course, different kinds of recurrence in Western music, and we should beware monolithic, totalizing theoretical models, as Scott Burnham rightly reminds us in his consideration of the grand subject of recurrence in sonata form: 'Return can be a moveable feast, and loose ends can encourage a welcome form of lightness, the loose weave of human possibility.'[15] The broad principle shared by Meyer and Schoenberg (and, let it be said, music theory going back centuries) is, though, one that makes intuitive sense to all, an intersubjective truth about musical structure.

The musical parallels between poetic and musical reiteration being rather clear in the kind of generalized way I am discussing here – and bearing in mind that this subject will arise again in various guises during the course of this book – I can turn without ceremony to the opposite of parallels, to lines that look as though they are heading in the same direction, but do not meet

---

[13] Leonard Meyer, *Emotion and Meaning in Music*, Chicago, University of Chicago Press, 1956, 152.

[14] Arnold Schoenberg, 'Construction of Themes', in *Fundamentals of Musical Composition*, London, Faber, 1970, 1–118. See also Jonathan Dunsby, 'Thematic and Motivic Analysis', in *The Cambridge History of Western Music Theory*, ed. Thomas Christensen, Cambridge, Cambridge University Press, 2002, 907–26, in particular the section on Schoenberg and 'developing variation', 911–16.

[15] Scott Burnham, 'The Second Nature of Sonata Form', in *Music Theory and Natural Order from the Renaissance to the Early Twentieth Century*, ed. Suzannah Clark and Alexander Rehding, Cambridge, Cambridge University Press, 2001, 111–41; 140.

even at infinity (the classic, geometrical definition of parallel lines being that they do meet at infinity, and not before). The divergence between poetic sense and musical structure is spectacular in general, although hard to grasp, as we shall discover, at the theorized levels of '-isms' and '-ologies'. At the level of making sense of everyday experience, the divergence is nevertheless apparent, if slippery to capture. Sticking just to the feature of reiteration, consider these remarkable lines (1 and 2) of a poem by Heinrich Heine from his collection *Lyrisches Intermezzo* of 1823:

> I bear no grudge, even though my heart may break,
> Eternally lost love! I bear no grudge.

> Ich grolle nicht und wenn das Herz auch bricht,
> Ewig verlor'nes Lieb, ich grolle nicht.

We can notice the sheer economy here poetically: there is already an implied epic history in the first line (why the heartbreak? and what made the poet first say, heartbroken, that it was all nevertheless grudgeless?); then a three-word cry from the heart that opens up further questions (how does the poet know this love is lost eternally, and do we instinctively and however fleetingly feel, then, that we may be in the presence of death? – well, the rest of the poem is rather unpleasant in its brief, stinging accusations and seems to tell us, for example in the last line, 'I saw, my love, how very miserable you are', that the 'I' in this poem is at the moment perhaps bitter after all, perhaps protesting too much). Then – in the lines above – there is a repetition ('I bear no grudge'), all the more prominent for taking up space in a compact environment where clearly space is at a premium, not a word wasted; a repetition that is easy to understand if we imagine the voice of someone perhaps talking to himself, not necessarily making the best of sense formally, except that the poet is making excellent sense in clearly *needing* to say something again that we (here is in one respect the poet's genius!) overhear – 'I bear no grudge' – which was, after all, a message that came through loud and clear in the first three words. Whatever you may think about my attempt to talk about Heine's opening words, Schumann's version of them for his 1840 Song 7 of *Dichterliebe* makes little sense as (verbal) poetry, and of course is not designed to do so:

> I bear no grudge, even though my heart may break,
> Eternally lost love, eternally lost love, I bear no grudge, I bear no grudge.

It is a musical stroke of genius (I deliberately use that word again) at this moment of a masterpiece, the song 'Ich grolle nicht', within the masterpiece that is *Dichterliebe*. How so? Firstly, music – tonal music at least – offers us

Ex. 1.1: Schumann, *Dichterliebe*, 'Ich grolle nicht', opening

sequence, and at 'x' in Ex. 1.1 the singer could (almost) hum or enunciate '*la*-la-la-*la*-la-*la*' for all that the semantics matter.

Secondly, at 'y' the music returns to the tonic (C major) and the melody completes its descending line back to the note E in a glorious dramatization of the poet's interior monologue: to ask whether Schumann got this right would be a little like asking whether Shakespeare allocated the correct number of iterations of the repeated word 'never' to the fading King Lear – one thing we expect of our 'geniuses' is that their touch does not falter, and then actors, or musical performers, have to work as best they can to that grain, to what is inscribed, enshrined by the composer, to the artistic 'writ' that plays such a prominent role in the value systems of Western art .

Two provisos here, one brief and one that needs expansion. Briefly, has the Trojan horse already appeared, in the above little analysis? I would say not, in that where a musical feature is judged to be definitive, then it becomes part of the vocal-musical fabric and must not be ignored. Reiteration is not, as Kivy has pointed out, obligatory, but where it occurs in a foundational way it must be ignored neither by philosophers – whom he accuses – nor also by commentators, critics, analysts:

> The importance of the repeat, both external and internal, in the music of this tradition cannot be overestimated, and has been not merely underestimated, but almost totally ignored by those who have tried to write 'philosophically' about such music. Indeed, I would put it this strongly: The music which I have been discussing does not merely contain repetition as an important feature, but as a defining feature.[16]

Secondly, and more significantly here, not only is musical reiteration, whether it is linked to words or is purely instrumental reiteration, 'absolute', of a different order from poetic reiteration, as my example above attempts to put over, but 'poetic language' – a term I used above, planted, without comment – is something we must look at more closely in any case. My thesis, on this particular aspect of how words are made to sing, is that poetic language is *not* the same as musical language, as will already be clear, and as will unfold in these pages again and again. It is hardly an original thesis – poetic language bears endless, fascinating comparison with music[17] – but in the end we are always conscious that just like our symmetrical left and right hands that work so intimately together, one thing is nevertheless one thing, and the other the other. This otherness – which we have already encountered in Chua's understandable awestruck characterization of the gulf between the instrumental and the vocal – resides in categorical distinctions.

Most obviously – and this is what has been most frequently and by and large most clearly discussed in the literature, as far as I am aware – verbal language means something. The ultramodernists of the mid twentieth

---

[16] Kivy, *The Fine Art of Repetition*, 359.
[17] And not merely in a casual sense, but for example as a deeply enshrined belief among the founders of modern linguistics, Roman Jakobson and Umberto Eco among them.

century knew this very well: Paul Celan, for example, writing in German, or Samuel Beckett in French and English. Take the beginning of the Beckett poem 'Serena II':

> this clonic earth
> see-saw she is blurred in sleep
> she is fat half dead the rest is free-wheeling
> part the black shag the pelt
> is ashen woad
> snarl and howl in the wood wake all the birds
> hound the harlots out of the ferns
> this damfool twilight threshing in the brake
> bleating to be bloodied
> this crapulent hush
> tear its heart out[18]

Whatever else he is up to here, Beckett is without doubt making sense. There are some obscure words (it's an Irish habit, alive to this day in the poetry of the ubiquitous Seamus Heaney), and you have to think hard about what belongs to what, but in fact any one of us who decided to punctuate this text conventionally would come up with pretty much the same making of sense: you'd have to be out of left field to reinscribe the last two lines of the extract as, say, 'This! Crapulent hush tear. Its; heart out', or some other such jabber (which may in its turn be rather interesting, of course). What Beckett's hush belongs to and why it is called crapulent, and what is having its heart torn out – those are other questions that we may wish to think about if we find the poem enticing and worth the effort.

Noam Chomsky theorized beautifully, if controversially to this day, the fundamental making of sense that language carries out with our cooperation as readers, a process with which we are all familiar in reading poetry. The supposedly weird sentence 'colourless green ideas sleep furiously' appeared as long ago as 1957 in his book *Syntactic Structures* and has been written about many times since. Its lesson, one that many find to be an alienating temptation often overexploited in the name of 'modernism', is that anything in a language *can* be understood as meaningful.[19] And of course

---

[18] *Poems in English by Samuel Beckett*, New York, Grove Press, 1961, 38.
[19] Typically one might be encouraged to think of those 'ideas' as bulbs underground in the winter. See also p. 87 for a reference to Barthes's idea of the 'prattle' of meaning. The kinds of 'Convention and Naturalization' that Barthes partly has in mind form an excellent chapter in Jonathan Culler's *Structuralist Poetics: Structuralism, Linguistics and the Study of Literature*, Ithaca, Cornell University Press, 1975, Chapter 7, 131–60. Culler is also the author of *Literary Theory: A Very Short Introduction*, Oxford, Oxford University Press, 1997, which includes a splendid, brief consideration of what 'literature' is and how it can be understood as meaningful, 17–39.

psychotheorists of the twentieth century caught and surfed this wave exultantly, in a wonderful hermeneutical funfair where everyone really could win a prize. Just where to locate such meaningfulness, it hardly needs to be said, is anything but self-evident. Witness only one corner of the extensive field of studies of Dickinson's poetry,[20] where we find the following brief but highly persuasive critique of John Cody's psychoanalytical search[21] for Dickinson's 'meanings':

The reason why Cody's psychoanalytic terminology all too often marginalizes the *trouvailles* found in his study seems to derive from two facts: (1) the univocal and technical discourse of psychoanalysis cannot do justice to *the multisemantic discourse of art*, and (2) the search of the biographer for real-life referents (with life as the primary text) truncates the richness of poetic language that raises personal experience onto a transpersonal and intersubjective level. In trying to interpret a literary text, psychoanalytic terminology is decidedly inferior to the critical discourse that embeds a work of art in its wider literary and sociocultural context, letting the network of meanings unfold through *the different layers of theme and form.*[22]

On these premises, then, those of reiteration and meaningfulness, I want to turn away from the initial implicit model here – an innocent implication, I trust, for the purposes of preliminary exposition – of the neutral text. For the text, any text, is *not* neutral, and this contention introduces a second category of 'otherness' in our understanding of the different worlds inhabited by language and by language in music, for language knows its own mind. Linguists were not wrong to point to the potential of any text to be meaningful, and this is the best way to understand the structuralist urge under the drive of which they were writing so perceptively. This urge was to proliferate in the work of Jacques Derrida in particular, but also in general in the post-1960s recognition that meaning exists as a function of its observers, and of course its users as observers. Much as we may revel in the pleasures of 'deconstructing' this meaning, however, there has to be a 'we' there in the first place.[23] It follows, so some leading thinkers believe,

---

[20] Cf. Chapter 6 for more detailed discussion of that field.
[21] See Chapter 6, note 1.
[22] Roland Hagenbüchte's chapter on 'Dickinson and Literary Theory', in G. Grabher et al., *The Emily Dickinson Handbook*, Amherst, University of Massachusetts Press, 1998, 356–84; 365–6 (my emphasis). It also hardly needs to be said that many psychoanalytical theorists would vigorously resist such a characterization of their discipline, although perhaps not so vigorously when it comes to the application of what might be called literary-critical 'would-be', rather than psychoanalytical actual techniques.
[23] For a lucid account and critique of deconstruction, see Christopher Butler, *Interpretation, Deconstruction, and Ideology: An Introduction to Some Current Issues in Literary Theory*, Oxford, Clarendon Press, 1984.

that there is a 'we' prior to verbal language, prior in evolutionary terms almost certainly,[24] but enduringly prior in the sense in which we ourselves can understand human consciousness in our own present, regardless of the history of our species. As Antonio Damasio puts it, in the terminology of an authority on the neurophysiology of consciousness:

> Language – that is, words and sentences – is a translation of something else, a conversion from non-linguistic images which stand for entities, events, relationship, and inferences. If language operates for the self and for consciousness in the same way that it operates for everything else, that is, by symbolizing in words and sentences what exists first in a nonverbal form, then *there must be a nonverbal self and a nonverbal knowing for which the words 'I' or 'me' or the phrase 'I know' are the appropriate translations*, in any language. I believe it is legitimate to take the phrase 'I know' and deduce from it the presence of a nonverbal image of knowing centred on *the self that precedes and motivates* that verbal phrase.[25]

The point I am trying to get to quickly is that all language, all text, carries a trace of this prior agency: it is not just a matter of things meaning what we decide they should mean or what we slip into thinking they mean: but that everything we encounter in verbal language did mean something in the first place; it always had and has *agency*.

Now this key point is a feature of our lives that will of course loom in and zoom out of our consciousness, but it seems to me one essential point of departure for what it may mean to make words sing, thinking first that this 'what' is about the words (although it seems more than likely that vocality preceded language in human evolution).[26] An example of our focusing on it is when we are trying to interpret hidden information, say the little phrase isolated in quotation marks, and signed, among Nietzsche's unpublished manuscripts, 'I have forgotten my umbrella', pounced upon, after having

---

[24] See for example Steven Mithen, *The Prehistory of the Mind: A Search for the Origins of Art, Religion and Science*, London, Thames and Hudson, 1996.

[25] Antonio Damasio, *The Feeling of What Happens: Body, Emotion and the Making of Consciousness*, London, Vintage, 2000, 107–8 (my emphasis).

[26] See for example Nicholas Bannan, 'The Role of the Voice in Human Development', PhD dissertation, University of Reading, 2002. Nietzsche, in 'On Music and Words' (see note 4), registers his strong view shared with Schopenhauer that music always arose linked to lyrical language 'long before there [could] be any thought of absolute music' in any human society (ibid., 107), but this was before debate about the history of the species had really got going. Charles Darwin himself was avowedly ignorant about the role of music in primitive human evolution, as is plain enough from Chapter 4 of *The Expression of the Emotions in Man and Animals*, London, John Murray, 1904, 2nd ed.; see especially 86–91, where he refers, however, to the mid-nineteenth-century evolutionary musical speculations of Herbert Spencer. Darwin's reluctance to pursue the question of the origins of music is perhaps naturally reflected in two modern, Darwin-oriented, 'popular' (but very serious) texts: Steve Jones, *Almost Like a Whale*: The Origin of Species *Updated*, London, Doubleday, 1999; and Adam Phillips, *Darwin's Worms*, London, Faber, 1999.

been omitted by the editors of Nietzsche's collected writings, in Derrida's rich account of the meaning that can be teased out of the epistemological tissue generated by the existence of this fragment.[27] In music our attention might turn to the repeated word '*ewig*' at the conclusion of Mahler's *Das Lied von der Erde* ('ever', as opposed to Lear's 'never'), which through repetition and isolation tends to lose its actual singer and gain a question about its human authorship and intention – no doubt Mahler was seeking to summon up the ultimately interrogative in this final completed music of his. We zoom out when, for example, there are bigger fish to fry: 'When I am laid, am laid in earth . . .', Purcell's Dido sings, so memorably and also vastly more often out of context in 'aria' guise than in her opera plot, '. . . remember me' – as if there were any remote chance that we might forget? As if it were entirely normal to have an audience one has never met being invited to remember one upon one's known and imminent death? As if Dido wants not only the relevant people on stage in her fictional world to remember her but also, clearly – and even if only out of context – *you* to do so, and me? Even though we do not customarily worry about this almost confusing network of questions, and the potential questions not articulated here, it is evident on reflection that the 'intentionality' of any text is not something we can ultimately hope to escape.

'Everything we encounter in verbal language did mean something in the first place' implies a certain degree of autonomy of any text, and this is I think precisely what Roland Barthes signals repeatedly in his writings, of which a choice instance is as follows:

> All writing will . . . contain the ambiguity of an object which is both language and coercion: There exists fundamentally in writing a 'circumstance' foreign to language[;] there is, as it were, the weight of a gaze conveying an intention which is no longer linguistic. This gaze may well express a passion of language, as in literary modes of writing; it may also express the threat of retribution, as in political ones . . . The word becomes an alibi, that is, an elsewhere and a justification.[28]

Assume that by 'coercion' Barthes would allow what I meant above by 'prior'. He is after all in this piece writing about 'Political Modes of Writing', so there is naturally a certain slant in his own language, of which as a brilliant – and that must always mean confident – writer he was well aware. It

[27] Jacques Derrida, *Spurs: Nietzsche's Styles*, Chicago, University of Chicago Press, 1979, 123–43. Derrida begins with such – to him – obvious questions as why did Nietzsche write this fragment? and perhaps even more indicatively, why did he sign it? The questions do, of course, develop during Derrida's study into more overtly complex philosophical and psychological ones.

[28] Roland Barthes, *Writing Degree Zero*, New York, Hill and Wang, 1968, 20.

amounts, this prior entity, he tells us, to a *gaze*, that favoured image of a certain Parisian theorizing of the later twentieth century. It is an image I want to emphasize, for after all Barthes was repeatedly pilloried as a champion of postmodern laissez-faire in a way that amounts to a wilful misunderstanding of his clearly stated intentions and beliefs, a misunderstanding to which he laid himself wide open as imaginative critics hovering on the borders of ideologies typically do.[29]

The *gaze* of the text is something that composers live with every day. They are the least likely people to forget it. Even in those strophic songs of Schubert where the music is apparently much better suited to the first stanza than following ones, this tells us something about the focus of his compositional attention in a certain concept of a certain type of Lied in the context of his contemporaneous aesthetic environment. We would be quite wrong to generalize from it, superficially, that Schubert took a cavalier approach to certain poetry – the text always has some price to pay for being set to music, and who is to say (I mean, where has the aesthetic argument ever been rigorously set out?) that the one or another of Schubert's strophic verses pays a 'greater' price than does a Heine lyric more subtly adapted by Schumann, and it, too, with its gaze stamped in the musical object? Or, conversely, that a text radically unpicked – as sometimes, for instance, in the hands of a Berio or a Boulez – makes any less 'sense', loses its 'gaze' more, than Schiller's 'Ode to Joy' sung in Beethoven's Ninth Symphony to the rightly celebrated theme that is nevertheless almost entirely in crotchets, almost as if the poem, contrary to the prevailing German aesthetic of the time, were in spoken Japanese with equally spaced syllables?

A third and for now final 'otherness' – substance – may already have occurred to the reader, and if not, this will be only because the temporal status of any object that appears to have what the word 'substance' implies is so very self-evidently 'other' than the insubstantial, passing, ephemeral 'content' of music. Words seem more 'substantial' than music, on the face of it, in that, for example, they tend to predate the music in which they may end up. It can of course happen the other way round – commonly, in the way that popular music is composed, where often the 'riff' and particularly the so-called 'hook' (melodic, harmonic, rhythmic, textural) may be the initial invention for which words need to be found; and idealistically, as

---

[29] For an example of textbook enshrinement of such misunderstanding, see Watkins, *Pyramids at the Louvre*, 469–70. Watkins's only quotation from Barthes in his whole book does not on careful reading support in the least the point he wants to make about an 'exaggerated objectivity and subjectivity in tandem with rampant cerebralism and irrationalism' – to the extent that one can even understand such an overstated position.

we shall see, in some Classical contexts. What comes first, however, tells us nothing about epistemological priority, and in any case we are not looking at priorities here but distinctions, differences. So we can let other forums, in music aesthetics, philosophy and psychology, concern themselves with the undoubted fact that music is as ephemeral as we can imagine an art to be.

UNTHEORY

It is difficult to marshal the main reasons why there has not been and does not seem likely to have been a 'theory of vocal music', which is, the moment one articulates it, a somewhat odd formulation – specialists coming from various differing musicological orientations would immediately be asking themselves what such a theory could possibly be about, what it might be at all like (see also Introduction, p. 6). Not that this situation has been without its irony: why, we might ask, in the 'modern' Romantic age of poetry and song, the nineteenth century, was theory almost devoid of widespread discussions of the nature of vocality?[30]

One can also be much more specific about the general point. In 1885 the great Viennese musicologist Guido Adler published an article on 'The Scope, Method and Aim of Musicology' that must count as one of the most majestic overviews of a discipline in the modern history of ideas.[31] Famously, and definingly, he divided musicology into the 'historical' and the 'systematic'. It is fair to say that what we think of as 'theory' (not least thanks to Adler) comes under the 'systematic'.[32] 'Vocality', as it is being called here, the resonances of the meaning of which are, it is hoped, gradually emerging, is essentially missing (there will be further discussion of those resonances throughout this book, but particularly near the beginning of Chapter 3). Adler lists 'dominating principles' of systematic musicology, but under melody we find only 'fusion of the *tonal* and *temporal*',[33] which is quintessential in Western music, but also anchored within that Trojan horse mentioned above: it is rampantly transvocal. Certainly Adler was not making any sort of mistake. He is, however, emblematic of his times

---

[30] See for example *Music Theory in the Age of Romanticism*, ed. Ian Bent, Cambridge, Cambridge University Press, 1996, an excellent 'reader' for its topic, which testifies to this point virtually throughout. Looking at the wider historical canvas, see similarly *The Cambridge History of Western Music Theory*, ed. Thomas Christensen, Cambridge, Cambridge University Press, 2002.

[31] See Guido Adler, 'The Scope, Method and Aim of Musicology', in *Music in European Thought 1851–1912*, ed. Bojan Bujic, Cambridge, Cambridge University Press, 1988, 348–55.

[32] See his 'tabular survey', ibid., 355.

[33] My emphasis.

and ideas. It was Adler who, I think, gave me the idea of the neologistic subtitle 'untheory' for this section – causing no offence, I trust, in the hope of putting forward a potentially useful term for areas that have been, previously in the musicological literature, more unseen than distrusted – when he simply refuses to take vocality seriously even in his peripheral, let alone central, vision, despite the brilliant cards in his hand (he was without doubt one of the more imaginative and knowledgeable musicologists of modern times), and despite the fact that at the very moments he was penning his wise words Brahms, for one, was writing his late Lieder. He is, like many a more modern theorist, deeply sceptical about aligning narrative with musical 'language': 'Even if the composer has used a poetic scheme – whether a programme or a general idea – it will be a bold man [*sic*] who will undertake to explain in musicologically acceptable terms the emotional content of the two component elements – musical and literary – and to demonstrate where they coincide and where they diverge.' And when it comes to music and actual words, he is a protostructuralist of whom a Roman Jakobson or a Claude Lévi-Strauss could have been entirely proud: 'Should there be an accompanying text, this must be critically examined – in the first place simply as poetry, then with regard to underlay and musical setting. Care must be taken to examine the accentuation and prosody in relation to the rhythms of the music; and this study of the text will provide further valuable assistance in coming to conclusions about the work.'[34]

Devotion to structure – and this is what I meant by being specific about the general point here – inevitably 'untheorizes' vocal music *as* vocal music, as what Jean-Jacques Nattiez means by a symbolic 'fact' compared with some vaguely posited empirical 'thing'.[35] Vocal music in Chua's sense of that magical presence simply floats free of the reductive in all its forms. I suppose this is why, so it would seem, psychoanalysis has barely touched it in the past hundred years, although 'song', say, is such an obvious candidate for the psychoanalytical mill in the sense that some supposedly structured entity (music) can be accessed via drives and meanings evident in narratives (poems, for example, not unlike life stories and, of course, especially recollected dreams); one may be impressed by psychoanalysis as a discipline for having largely stayed away from this elusive territory.

If one were to ask why 'untheory' were of interest, with its negative and unproductive connotations, among various possible answers I would opt for the underlying one that derives from the French eighteenth-century

[34] Ibid., 350 and 349 respectively.
[35] Jean-Jacques Nattiez, *Music and Discourse: Toward a Semiology of Music*, Princeton, Princeton University Press, 1990; see for example 196.

view, revitalized by, for instance, Michel Foucault recently, that what is different is best understood from its authentic source. Anything worth studying will demand some degree of interiority in that it must always demand an attention to what it is, as well as to what it does. I believe it is not to misrepresent Jürgen Habermas, an extremely sophisticated, complex philosopher, to quote directly and without comment on this point at least:

> Hermeneutic understanding can never analyze the structure of its object to the point of eliminating all contingency. Otherwise it would turn into reconstruction, that is, understanding the meaning of formal relations . . . Because we are not in possession of such rules of reconstruction for traditional meaning structures, they require a hermeneutic understanding of meaning that apprehends symbolic relations as relations of fact. *Hermeneutics* is both a form of experience and grammatical analysis at the same time.[36]

So why, for example, of all people – think of the most radical composer since, say, Wagner, of one so wedded to words that he spent maybe half his life writing them alongside writing music, who had a long and productive career in which he returned to vocality again and again as a champion of new art – why of all people did Schoenberg 'untheorize' what it was to make words sing? It is instructive, for example, to ponder in Schoenberg the almost complete lack of reference to vocal music, to text/music issues, even to the conventional imprints of vocality in general music theory such as so-called 'song' form, 'refrain' structure and the like. Not that Schoenberg consistently fails to discuss such phenomena – on the contrary, there are remarkable contributions both general (as in the essay 'The Relationship to the Text',[37] originally published in the almanac *Der blaue Reiter* of 1912) and specifically regarding the compositional process (as in Schoenberg's 'Self-analysis').[38] The fact remains, though, that in Schoenberg's sustained attempt to formulate a theory of musical 'coherence' (his favoured word for his theoretical ideal) during the 1920s and 1930s (partly published, and thoroughly documented, only as recently as during the past decade),[39] he found it to all appearances completely unnecessary to make a special case for music/text issues. Most of his musical examples in *The Musical Idea* are from the nonvocal repertoire; and when he does cite such a classic

---

[36] Jürgen Habermas, *Knowledge and Human Interests*, Oxford, Polity Press [1968], 1987, 161–2.
[37] Arnold Schoenberg, *Style and Idea: Selected Writing of Arnold Schoenberg*, London, Faber, 1975, 141–5.
[38] Willi Reich, *Schoenberg: A Critical Biography*, Harlow, Longman, 1971, 236–42 (Appendix 1).
[39] Arnold Schoenberg, *The Musical Idea and the Logic, Technique, and Art of its Presentation*, ed. and trans. Patricia Carpenter and Severine Neff, New York, Columbia University Press, 1993.

melody as Puccini's 'E lucevan le stelle' from *Tosca*[40] the words of the aria
are neither written into the music example nor mentioned. It is certainly
possible to overreact to such relatively isolated pieces of evidence, and it
would be ludicrous to imagine that a composer whose own oeuvre focused
repeatedly on new challenges in word/music relations – from the 2nd String
Quartet (1908) and *Pierrot lunaire* to *Moses und Aron* and the *Modern Psalm*
(1950) – was anything other than continually thinking about them. Still,
Schoenberg is outspoken in the 1931 'Self-analysis':

> I always used to look for a particular poem, and often, certainly its content (mood
> and emotions) had to match preconceived ideas of my own. All the same, I often
> ended up by choosing something quite different, perhaps because it matched a
> musical idea that was in my mind; a theme, waiting for someone to help it into
> the world . . . To sum up: the words are often an occasion, an excuse, a stimulus.
> What really draws me to them is my musical need.[41]

This chimes in with sentiments expressed recurrently by Schoenberg. The
text is, he usually seems to feel, a 'pretext', both in the sense of it having
an enabling function, but also in the sense of being the prior form of
its eventual transformation into a literally unprecedented musicopoetic
object, if we may take a simple lead for the moment from Edward Cone's
idea of the composer as poet[42] – taking possession of a text in a way that
essentially severs its connection with the literary original. He shared the
belief in transvocality that guarantees a comfortable interplay between the
verbal and the music. So when, for instance, he wrote in 1912, having
been asked by his publisher to supply titles for each of the Five Orchestral
Pieces, Op. 16, 'If words were needed they would be there already. But
anyways music says more than words', it is an indication of *control*, not
theoretical puzzlement, of being at ease with the multifaceted nature of the
art of music. Similarly, when he comments on a performance of some of
his songs and especially the *George-Lieder*, Op. 15, by the singer Marta
Winternitz-Dorda, whose ability and artistry he greatly admired in general,
'Much too dramatic (rather ordinary), everything shaped by word rather
than music. In a word: the usual style nowadays', he signals not only perhaps
his understanding of the singer's motivations as an interpreter, but also his

---

[40] Ibid., 193. There is a wrong note in the fourth full bar of this example – E for F sharp on beats 1 and
2 – which is a trivial matter whatever its aetiology.

[41] Reich, *Schoenberg*, 240.

[42] See for example, from Cone's various writings in this respect, the essay 'Poet's Love or Composer's
Love?', in *Music and Text: Critical Inquiries*, ed. Stephen Scher, Cambridge, Cambridge University
Press, 1992, 177–92.

clear awareness of an alternative, of an ideal balance between the forces of text and those of transvocal interpretation.[43]

Does this mean that there is no place, in the modern Western musical tradition, for musicopoetic theorizing, for the identification of principles in what happens when words are, as we say, 'set to' music, assimilated by it (to follow Schoenberg's feeling), reinvented (to follow Cone at one stage of his writings)? Most commentators, as I understand it, would answer 'yes'. 'To look for epochal changes with respect to the combination of music and words', wrote William Austin,[44] 'we need to keep in mind *the whole range of perplexing interrelations* . . . A mere assembly of observations, very loosely organized, may be as useful as any theory, impressing us with the sheer variety of composers' practices and perhaps increasing our sympathy with their various efforts.'[45]

So it is not out of theoretical pessimism, but in the spirit of a celebration of musical practice that I suggest now leaving behind 'untheory' and carrying forward the ideas of transvocality (including its seductive critical dangers) and the 'intentionality' of the text into the investigation of compositional practices crossing the past two centuries. Inevitably this will in part amount to a series of windows on to the forming of, reforming of and resistance to Modernism.

REVIEW

We will find, especially in the detailed case studies in the following chapters, that those 'critical dangers' mentioned above often amount to issues of language. Kramer, again, with his fine ability to encapsulate issues, aims to remind us, as I understand it, that interpretation – or hermeneutical discourse to give it what may be its best tag – is not an unmediated phenomenon, it has no hotline to some supposedly pure and uncluttered wellspring of human comprehension. 'Language', writes Kramer, 'cannot capture musical experience because it cannot capture any experience whatever, including the experience of language itself.'[46] This is in the context

---

[43] Arnold Schoenberg, *Berliner Tagebuch*, Frankfurt am Main, Propyläen Verlag, 1974, 14 and 19 respectively (my translations). His 'word . . . in a word' is either a deliberate pun, or clumsy – or perhaps both, in this diary that does anything but reflect Schoenberg's customary outstanding polish as a writer.

[44] William Austin, 'Words and Music: Theory and Practice of 20th- Century Composers', in *Words and Music: The Composer's View*, ed. Lawrence Berman, Cambridge, Mass., Harvard University Press, 1971, 1–8; 1.

[45] Ibid., 3 (my emphasis).

[46] Lawrence Kramer, *Classical Music and Postmodern Knowledge*, Berkeley, University of California Press, 1995, 18.

of a discussion of 'Postmodernism and Musicology' (1–32) where Kramer
seems to be inviting us to abandon the categorical distinctions, the 'universal principles', of 'formalism and positivism' (33) in favour of an altogether
more personally oriented musicology (these are my words) in which the
'alterity' of the self is, in the spirit of the zeitgeist of the 1980s, a pervasive,
awe-inspiring symbol.

There is always something 'other' about our experience of the world
and so an art-form such as ensemble song ought to be a hermeneutical paradise with its patent array of alterities, most notably text/music,
voice/instrument(s), but with other deep-seated combinations of forces
such as have been discussed in the preceding pages (vocality/transvocality,
language/agency, semantic/poetic, semantic/musical). In discussing music
without words, I wanted to establish that there is a certain hegemony of
musicostructural concerns in this study in general. There is no intention to
claim the discovery somehow of a new critical nirvana where the language
of music and the language of language have become miraculously so inter-
penetrating that they are no longer epistemologically distinct. On the other
hand, song does simply resist our deep organicist urges, which have often
been squabbled about in rather futile discussion (mainly, it has seemed, by
those whose critical agendas simply do not intersect with the mainstream of
Western music theory, as they are perfectly well entitled not to do), but to
which urges it ought to be at least possible to consider alternatives of some
sort that do not go so far as to deny them. This is the line taken in Robert
Fink's thoughtful essay 'Going Flat: Post-Hierarchical Music Theory and
the Musical Surface': 'making a totality-machine out of music', he writes,
'does powerful cultural work: it provides a way of reinforcing the bounded,
interior self, perpetually under attack in modern and postmodern society',
but, he asks, 'what if we relieve music of this burden, and choose to con-
ceptualise and experience musical artworks as pure desiring-machines?'[47]
As Fink well knows, it is much easier to conceive of this in looking at some
music of the late twentieth century, especially the ravishing world of the
so-called minimalists, than the more established repertoire considered in
detail here, yet the aspiration is one well worth bearing in mind, and in the
traditions of discussing music and text the 'totality-machine' approaches –
looking for literal correspondences between note and word, looking for
an idealized unity of poetic conception, looking for some kind of elusive 'third' language that, if it exists, we can be sure is completely,

---

[47] Robert Fink, 'Going Flat: Post-Hierarchical Music Theory and the Musical Surface', in *Rethinking
   Music*, ed. Nicholas Cook and Mark Everist, Oxford, Oxford University Press, 1999, 102–37; 136.

categorically beyond description, let alone analysis – have been the least satisfying.

In discussing 'intended words', similarly, the idea has been to try to suspend the utterly seductive notion of the 'death of the author' not in the interests of some prurient biographical urge or to fall back into the comforting arms of the composer's intention (for they always slip away just when one seems to need their support) but because the ascetic primitivism of the structuralist urge fails us miserably when it comes to some of the most interesting, most human aspects of song. If that ascetic primitivism is in part at least what Kramer means by 'formalism', then his call for it to be stepped over deserves anyone's support. One cannot but notice that, for example, such a flagship of structuralism as the widely anthologised critical analysis of Baudelaire's poem 'Les chats' in Jakobson's and Lévi-Strauss's neutral 'decomposition' of a complex symbolist poem is not only anything but neutral – one wants to reach for a term such as 'neutralistic' by analogy with Richard Taruskin's term 'authenticist' for the reconstructions of supposedly authentic performance practice[48] – but is on a poem about, well, cats. More impressive might have been some structuralist surgery on a poem as semantically opaque and humanly engaged as Dickinson's 'Going to Heaven' (see Chapter 5), and there would be nothing wrong with the attempt, but only if we were clear that this would be to privilege the neutral, structural aspects over the poietic, 'compositional' ones including the panoply of historical information, and to privilege them over our esthesic reception, that is, our rich and varied response to the work of art, and its place in the world, of which the composer can predict little and eventually know nothing.

In this delicate balance of intention and interpretation, a discussion of 'untheory' has been appropriate because of the need to flesh out Habermas's idea of hermeneutics, which undoubtedly involves what he calls grammatical analysis, but also and crucially, as he says, it involves a 'form of experience' (see p. 27). There is a tendency, which will be familiar to some readers, to assume that the citadels of Schenkerian analysis (see Chapter 2), and traditional formal analysis, as well as, say, pitch-class set theories, modal theory, rhetorical theory and perhaps a few other outposts, represent typical strongholds of theoretical kinship, power and influence. Yet the purview of music theory has always been rather small, and often seriously out of kilter with practice because it was either running ahead (as, for example, with

---

[48] See Taruskin's essay 'The Presence of the Past and the Pastness of the Present', in *Text and Act: Essays on Music and Performance*, Oxford, Oxford University Press, 1995, 90–154.

theories of pan- and post-tonality in the early nineteenth century, decades ahead of significant practice in this respect[49]) or running behind (today's relative lack of widespread, intensive technical study of musical composition of the past two or three decades may be an example). One commentator rightly mentions the 'fallacy of proximity', leading to a certain prejudice that 'presupposes a collective *Zeitgeist*, whereby coeval theories will necessarily be more "in tune" with the music of their time. A rudimentary knowledge of both music history and music theory makes it abundantly clear that this is as much the exception as it is the rule.'[50] When it comes to the analysis of song, and the general understanding of what goes into song and what we get out of it, the more familiar theoretical questions, even aside from those of historical proximity, are largely beside the point. It is difficult to imagine what a generic, structural theory of the Lied would be like, and what it would be for. One cannot but admit, then, that this field is condemned to what Kramer probably means by 'positivism' (see p. 30), the notion popularized as a critique of modern musicology by Joseph Kerman, the notion of ascertaining facts without a prior or at least provisional concept of how they are regulated, be it taxonomically or generatively.[51] It will already be clear even from the brief discussion in Part 3 of this chapter that 'untheory' is designed to offer a way to twist out of this old conundrum without our feeling the need to import other theories and external frames of reference as a kind of bailing-out procedure, without feeling the need to 'get out' of analysis as Kerman notoriously put it, and without accepting the 'New Musicology' misunderstandings of music-analytical practice based above all, as Kofi Agawu has forcefully argued, on ignorance.[52]

---

[49] I have written elsewhere of the 'inherent, multi-dimensional experimentalism that, far from creeping up on the closing decades of nineteenth-century music, was of its essence'. See Jonathan Dunsby, 'Chamber Music and Piano', in *The Cambridge History of Nineteenth-Century Music*, ed. Jim Samson, 500–21; 514.

[50] Thomas Christensen, 'Music Theory and Its Histories', in *Music Theory and the Exploration of the Past*, ed. Christopher Hatch and David Berstein, Chicago, University of Chicago Press, 1993, 1–39; 25.

[51] This line of critique runs through Joseph Kerman's *Musicology*.

[52] Kofi Agawu, 'Analyzing Music under the New Musicological Regime', in *Music Theory On-Line*, 2/4, May 1996 [accessed 29 February 2004].

CHAPTER 2

A love song: Brahms's 'Von ewiger Liebe'

'You'd think that people would have had enough' – wrote Paul McCartney, and more to the point he sang with his group Wings on record, in 1976, becoming an overnight world success – 'of silly love songs'. Enough of love songs; it's quite a thought. Whether one should be quoting a popular singer on the subject is open to question, scholarly question that is, in a study centring on Brahms; while on the other hand one imagines that if anyone is qualified to comment on song at least in the later twentieth century, it ought to be someone like McCartney who was the era's most globalized writer and performer of song. 'Classical' his song world may not be, but representative of the most widespread and highly valued form of vocality it certainly was.

Admittedly there is something painfully overindulgent in taking too forensic a view of popular culture – not that it fails to be as significant as any other kind of art, and from many points of view it is among the most important expressions of human sentiment, if important means sincere and, in the age of technology, truly widely shared, art of the people if ever there was one. It is always difficult to wonder how to evaluate the fleetingly memorable (deeply though popular art penetrates into our psyche) in comparison with art designed to be lasting; all too easy to give in to some form of cultural imperialism when we compare a work of supposedly 'high' art with something perceived to be its opposite – popular, improvisatory perhaps, laden with reference so contemporaneous that it is dated almost the moment it is produced, and in short therefore, dare one even write it, 'low'. Only in societies of extreme bigotry and insularity would such high/low comparisons seem easy and solved, as in Victorian England with its neurotic fear of the foreign, of the so-called 'primitive', or with its more introversive fear of, say, women composers that it shared with other European societies (thus some of Fanny Hensel's songs were published under the name of her brother Felix Mendelssohn, as much for gender reasons as reasons of reputation).[1]

Yet the inexorability of the interplay between the serious and something perceived to be less than serious is evident in the best-kept establishments. Witness Arnold Schoenberg's note of appreciation on the death of George Gershwin in 1937, the arch-serious modernist in the most ivory and towering of positions writing about the young songsmith superstar who had definitively wooed not only the great American public but all five continents with numbers such as 'I Got Rhythm' and 'Summertime' (the latter, incidentally, from an opera, *Porgy and Bess*, did the public but know it or care). 'Many musicians do not consider George Gershwin a serious composer', Schoenberg begins, and he ends thus: 'but I know he is an artist and a composer; he expressed musical ideas; and they were new – as is the way in which he expressed them'.[2] Touching that may be, but with all his good intentions Schoenberg cannot avoid little patronizing self-revelations during his short narrative, almost from the beginning when he tells us about what it is to be a composer expressing things that may be 'serious or not, sound or superficial'; and also in the elaboration of his argument when he notes that Gershwin gives the impression 'of an improvisation with all the merits and shortcomings appertaining to this kind of production' (not something Schoenberg ever seems to have written about Schubert's hundreds of songs that we suppose must have been in some sense 'improvised' and presumably thus also subject to 'shortcomings' of some kind); and specifically, weightily, in finally giving way to a failed attempt to deny cultural validation – 'I do not speak here as a musical theorist, nor am I a critic, and hence I am not forced to say whether history will consider Gershwin a kind of Johann Strauss or Debussy, Offenbach or Brahms, Lehár or Puccini' – Schoenberg has been drawn into comparisons that are deeply obscure chronologically, generically, geographically. What is more, the comments here have been somewhat spun in Schoenberg's favour, using the word 'songsmith' of Gershwin, for example, given that Schoenberg does not say exactly what music of Gershwin he is writing about. If he is thinking in a way that is meant to embrace not only the famous songs and the shows made up of songs, but also Gershwin's opera and a work such as the Piano Concerto, then Schoenberg will be seen to be capitulating to the inexorable forces of inadvertent cultural canonicity, since Gershwin certainly did try

[1] See Nancy Reich, 'Fanny Hensel: The Power of Class', in *Mendelssohn and His World*, ed. R. Larry Todd, Princeton, Princeton University Press, 1991, 86–99.
[2] Arnold Schoenberg, 'George Gershwin', in *Style and Idea: Selected Writing of Arnold Schoenberg*, London, Faber, 1975, 476–7.

far beyond his stereotype to be a contemplative, nonimprovisatory composer (to borrow Schoenberg's rhetoric for a moment), since many would say that he succeeded brilliantly, and since there is plenty of evidence to which they could point – for example, the number and variety of major 'classical' soloists who have made recordings of that concerto.

So however tempted we may be to think 'enough of silly love songs', we may also agree with McCartney's equally memorable next lines:

> But I look around me and I see it isn't so.
> Some people wanna fill the world with silly love songs.
> And what's wrong with that?
> I'd like to know, 'cause here I go again . . .

I guess that Brahms would have thought, and in his own way said, much the same as that. 'Von ewiger Liebe'[3] is not merely an austere contemplation on the nature of 'Love Eternal', to put it in a rather old-fashioned manner that would nowadays capture a sense of the venerated, of the grave, in a way that we might imagine of some inhibited Victorian composer, even a German one well used to the extremes of Romantic expression. On the contrary, one should have in mind that Brahms was, is, thinking about love going on for ever in a burning present that great art, serious or popular, can summon; or we can recall the English composer Roger Marsh's delightful and anything but flippant title from the McCartney era of a work for voice, clarinet and piano, 'Another Silly Love Song'.[4] Not least in a context such as the one here, where we shall be taking some deeply technical slices into Brahms's work, technical in the sense of trying to get to some of the essence of the musical processes underpinning the supreme vocality of 'Von ewiger Liebe', it is important to keep firmly in mind somewhere that Brahms really does mean this lovely story that, in a word, I would say is about the *certainty* of love, even if at the end of everything we shall have to say and think about it, 'Von ewiger Liebe' is, like Isolde's *Liebestod*, 'just' another love song. We do not need to ask here whether it would be right to cross the line between art and biography in supposing that Brahms was expressing his own experience through this setting in some usefully identifiable way, or whether there is some overall story to be told about this song in relation to two earlier love

---

[3] This song was published in 1868 as the first of the *Vier Gesänge*, Op. 43, on which Brahms had been working between about 1857 and 1866. The second song, 'Die Mainacht', on a poem by Hölty, is another magnificent little composition that has been discussed frequently in the critical literature on Brahms.

[4] Roger Marsh, 'Another Silly Love Song', London, Novello & Co. Ltd, 1976.

songs 'Treue Liebe', Op. 7, No.1 (1852) and 'Liebestreu', Op. 3, No. 1 (1853).[5] But there is no reason either to ignore its rather special place in the view of Brahms and of the Romantic Lied, to which generation after generation of critic has attested. Already in Max Kalbeck's biography of Brahms, the first comprehensive account of his life and works based on contemporaneous evidence and stemming from the very zeitgeist of Brahms's later life, 'Von ewiger Liebe' is picked out as 'perhaps the most famous and most often sung of Brahms's Lieder'.[6] A century or so later, A. Craig Bell remains transfixed by the technical accomplishment: 'No song even in Schubert is more spaciously conceived or designed than this nocturnal scene.'[7]

Von ewiger Liebe
Dunkel, wie dunkel in Wald und in Feld!
Abend schon ist es, nun schweiget die Welt.
Nirgend noch Licht und nirgend noch Rauch,
Ja, und die Lerche sie schweiget nun auch.

Kommt aus dem Dorfe der Bursche heraus,
Gibt das Geleit der Geliebten nach Haus,
Führt sie am Weidengebüsche vorbei,
Redet so viel und so mancherlei:

'Leidest du Schmach und betrübest du dich,
Leidest du Schmach von andern um mich,
Werde die Liebe getrennt so geschwind,
Schnell wie wir früher vereiniget sind.
Scheide mit Regen und scheide mit Wind,
Schnell wie wir früher vereiniget sind.'

Spricht das Mägdelein, Mägdelein spricht:
'Unsere Liebe sie trennet sich nicht!
Fest ist der Stahl und das Eisen gar sehr,
Unsere Liebe ist fester noch mehr.

---

[5] See Thomas Sick, '"Unsere Liebe muss ewig bestehn!": Liebestreue in Brahms' Liedschaffen', in *Brahms als Liedkomponist: Studien zum Verhältnis von Text und Vertonung*, ed. Peter Jost, Stuttgart, F. Steiner, 1992, 173–89, for one who does believe there is a connection, although he fails to spell out what it is in other than a general, inferable sense.
[6] Max Kalbeck, *Johannes Brahms*, Berlin, Deutsche Brahms-Gesellschaft, 1921, 3rd ed., 2, 129 (my translation).
[7] A. Craig Bell, *Brahms, The Vocal Music*, London, Associated University Presses, 1996, 71. For a reasonably reliable and recent short essay on this song, see Misha Donat, '4 Gesänge, Opus 43', in *The Compleat Brahms: A Guide to the Musical Works of Johannes Brahms*, ed. Leon Botstein, New York, Norton, 1999, 229–34. The origin of the girl's melody in a long-unpublished wedding chorus written by Brahms in Hamburg (in 1858, about a decade before 'Von ewiger Liebe') is mentioned in most secondary sources and can be studied (with a musical example illustrating the derivation) in, for example, the widely available book by Max Harrison, *The Lieder of Brahms*, London, Cassell, 1972, 78.

Eisen und Stahl, man schmiedet sie um,
Unsere Liebe, wer wandelt sie um?
Eisen und Stahl, sie können zergehn,
Unsere Liebe muß ewig bestehn!'

Of Eternal Love
Dark, how dark in the forest and field!
Night has already fallen, the world now is silent.
Nowhere any light and no trail of smoke,
And even the lark is silent now.

Coming from the village is a young man,
Taking his beloved to her home.
Leads her past the willow bushes,
Talks so much of so many things:

'If you suffer shame and it grieves you,
If you suffer shame from others because of me,
Then shall our love be ended as suddenly,
As fast as we once came together;
Dissolve in the rain and dissolve in the wind,
As fast as we once came together.'

Then says the girl, the girl says:
'Our love shall never end!
Steel is firm and iron is too,
Our love is even firmer.

Iron and steel, you can recast them,
But who could transform our love?
Iron and steel can melt;
Our love must last for ever!'[8]

This is a simple ballad. It was once thought to be, because of Brahms's own wrong ascription, a Wendish (also known as Sorbian, from Slavic Eastern Germany) folk lyric translated into German by Josef Wenzig, but eventually it became clear that it is the work of Heinrich Hoffman von Fallersleben.[9] In any case, the text was a characteristic kind of choice for

---

[8] My translation. The reader will easily locate more poetic translations of this poem including singing versions.

[9] Although the reader will not want to be detained over the detailed history of this corner of Brahms scholarship, it is nevertheless a fascinating footnote to historical musicology to observe the sheer authority of Brahms's error, which persisted for more than a century. I believe that the first question in modern times about the authorship of the poem 'Von ewiger Liebe' was raised in 1972 by Eric Sams in ' "Von ewiger Liebe" ', in *Neue Zeitschrift für Musik*, 133, 257, where he observed that the poem was not in fact to be found in the two volumes of Wenzig translations owned by Brahms, and anyway the poem itself lacked the supposed 'folk character' one would expect. Sams thought it much more likely to be the work of a gifted poet with whom Brahms was already familiar through Schumann's library and compositions, and indeed the poem was found in Fallersleben's 1837 *Gedichten*.

Brahms, who, for example, produced some forty-six songs on texts that were not even by canonically 'minor' poets but anonymous (including four from the Bible), and who, though willing to take on 'great' poems of a Goethe or a Mörike from time to time, took the view in general, in his output of some two hundred songs altogether, that music should be used only if it can enhance the poetry, something that is not likely to be an everyday occurrence. The poem is undoubtedly rather beautiful in German, with its lulling word repetitions ('Dunkel, wie dunkel . . . / Nirgend noch Licht und nirgend noch Rauch . . . / so viel und so mancherlei/ Leidest . . . Leidest, etc.), chiasmus ('Schnell–Scheide . . . Scheide–Schnell/ Stahl–Eisen . . . Eisen–Stahl), assonances and inner sound-matches ('*Gi*bt das *Gel*eit der *Gel*iebten'), and a rhyme scheme that binds not only pairs of lines, but approximately also lines 5–6 with 3–4, thus across the first two verses, and then lines 9–10 at the beginning of the third verse projected forward to lines 15–16 at the beginning of the fourth (dich . . . / mich . . . / spricht . . . / nicht). The poem also has a powerful dramatic 'plot', beginning with the landscape, dark and silent, then picking out the young man walking his beloved home and apparently talking volubly to her, then tuning in to what he is saying – it is the model of what would become a typical film shot as we focus in on the scenery, on the characters, and then on what they are saying. This overheard quality built in to the poem does lend a high degree of intimacy to the conversation beginning in verse 3, a moment of dramatic turning that Brahms will need to enhance in the music (if adding something to the poem). The final phase of the story is the beloved's reply, of touching simplicity and determination; as well as a remarkable immediacy, or realism, as she comes out not with some elegantly turned formal argument or flowery sentiment drawn from her knowledge of two thousand years of love poetry, but a heartfelt assertion of the moment, of an eternal moment.

We may want to ask two rather obvious lurking questions about this story. Firstly, what is wrong with this boy such that it seems obvious to him that his beloved might be picking up criticisms and disapproval of their relationship, and that if she is overly bothered by this then the agreement can simply be terminated forthwith? Secondly, is the female overstating the case, being neurotically defensive in some way, with her triumphant, timeless assertion of a particular love being more chemically stable than metals? But one might also ask when it is not possible to ask such cynical questions. They are probably best answered through an appeal to sincerity, since this kind of wilful overstatement, a black-and-white, unconditional reification of inner feeling is found to be typical of young love. It may not be for everyone, or within everyone's personal experience, but the genuineness of these direct and extreme positions is valid and evidenced in many centuries' worth of world literature, as in McCartney's song. In purely poetic terms the two-verse closing speech by the girl captures exquisitely human speech in its thought-process (not that in real life she would be likely to speak in rhyming couplets). She thinks three times about her idea, steel and iron, iron and steel. They are solid, but not as solid as our love: and thinking about this, you can reshape iron and steel, but who could reshape what we have together? And what is more, you know that iron and steel really can be melted, but our love, our love never, ever can be – it will last for ever. If such a paraphrase is almost nothing but a diminishing of the original, it can nevertheless give a sense of how close are these lines, which obviously must have fascinated Brahms for him to give them such close attention, to a real and magical moment of affirmation through words, and also to an urgent innocence that keeps our minds on the purely spiritual rather than engaging the body. It is a true theatre of the mind. Musically, what does Brahms do to transform this verbal high point, the girl's speech?

To anticipate for a moment later music-analytical readings of this music, we can at least note here the sheer simplicity of his solutions within his complex art-object. Firstly, he introduces a profound 'twist' to the phrasing. It is not that his proportional strategy has been straightforward all along, since the vocal regularity is embedded in phrase extensions from the piano, which set the folksong squareness of the melody into crystal relief. Hence, for example, the disposition of the first verse, where the piano's four-bar introduction is shown to be followed by overlapping regular phrases (of two and four bars respectively) producing, overall, the irregular nine (bars 5–13) plus eleven (bars 14–24) in the sense of the piano in bars 21–4 rounding off the first verse, although this material is also the introduction again, leading for verse 2 in the voice from bar 25:

bar:	1 2 3 4 5 6 7 8 9 10 11 12 13 14 15 16 17 18 19 20 21 22 23 24
voice:	└——— 8 ———┘ └——— 8 ———┘
piano:	└4┘ ·············· └2┘ ············· └— 4 —┘
verse:	1 2

Nevertheless, the delivery of narrative in 8 + 8 bars is as the diagram above clearly indicates. And this pattern continues in verse 3, where the three couplets are set in contiguous eight-bar phrases (bars 45–52, 53–60, 61–68). This triple regularity is a powerful form of articulation, which Brahms has taken straight from the poem, and it finds its resonance in the piano transition closing this section (bars 68ff., 70ff., 71ff.), although the proportional structure is perhaps best interpreted as an eight-bar unit (as established by the triple occurrence just mentioned) extended to nine, with a further two-bar extension. However that may be, the 'girl's speech' section, heralded by a change of mode (B minor to major) and time signature ($\frac{3}{4}$ to $\frac{6}{8}$), as well as in the musical material, sees the onset of another four-square vocal invention, in a textbook phrasing over bars 79–94 with piano once again providing an 'asymmetry' to offset the vocal periodicity:

```
voice:                                16
                        (8           +            8)
             (4       +      4)            (4       +      4)
            (2+2)          (2+2)          (2+2)          (2+2)
piano:                                                └─ 2 + 3 ─┘
```

Note that so far the voice has sung sixteen bars separated into two eight-bar phrases, and sixteen bars in two contiguous eight-bar phrases. All that Brahms does, 'all' that he needs to do (but one needs to have conceived the whole song in the first place), is extend the final vocal phrase so that what might have been a close something like Ex. 2.1.1 becomes the gloriously superabundant Ex. 2.1.2.

Ex. 2.1.1   Un - se - re Lie - be? muß e - wig be - stehn!"

Ex. 2.1.2   Un - se - re Lie - be,   un - se re Lie - be muß e - wig, e   -   wig be - stehn!"

Ex. 2.1: Brahms, 'Von ewiger Liebe', possible vocal ending and actual vocal ending

It will be noticed that here Brahms alters the text – the only place in his setting where he does – so that 'Unsere Liebe muss ewig bestehn' (word for word: 'our love must always continue') becomes the heightened version through repetition: 'Unsere Liebe, unsere Liebe muss ewig, ewig bestehn', which, incidentally, purely at the level of verbal poetry beautifully reflects the previous imprints of repetition in the original text, although I am not saying that was really Brahms's intention, focused as he certainly was on the vocality of the musicopoetic result and not merely on any reshaping of the poetry itself.[10] The 'shadow' version in Ex. 2.1.1, the unconscious structure of Brahms's own compositional ending if you like, takes its pitch information from the precedents in the song. The voice has never reached higher than the note E (one octave above middle C). E was used climactically in bar 66: the fourth degree of the scale on B (minor or major), it is fundamentally dissonant, will always fall to D (or D sharp), and will not be available to be used as a conclusive 'goal' of the vocal line (or it is highly unlikely). The F sharp lying above it, the fifth degree of the scale, has, however, been adumbrated an octave lower in the piano transition into the major section mentioned above (see bars 68ff.), which is taken up as a local 'pedal' note in the piano at the beginning of the major section, and which appears in its authentic octave (one octave above middle C) in bar 94. Everything is set up, in other words, for the voice eventually at bar 113 (see Ex. 2.1.2) to reach that long-heralded F sharp that in essence marks the end of Brahms's story for us.[11]

Harmonically, too, this closing passage is extraordinarily strong, and not least because of Brahms's fine sense of harmonic pace, in a song that has been characterized by sustained harmonic prolongations. To look at the last verse only (that is, the last four lines of text) we can see this acute apposition of the 'build-up' through relatively long harmonic steps:

Bar: 99 100 101 102 103 104 105 106 107 108 109 110 111 112
In B: I   IV   II   V

and a rapid, triumphant assertion of the diatonic scale-steps:

Bar: 113   114   115   116   117
In B: I   (III IV) II   (IV VII III VI II) V   I

Not that there is anything experimental or even progressive about that – similar examples, from the point of view of musical grammar, can be found throughout music of the preceding century and more. It is rather the coming together of these various structural forces allied to the piercing sentiments of the text that gives the whole an astonishing momentum that one could not predict from the naming of its parts.

---

[10] Sick mentions accurately enough that 'the melody of the whole song is articulated continuously in four-bar groups, each corresponding to a line of text. This procedure is interrupted in the last line . . . the phrase is extended to five and then seven bars.' See Sick, ' "Unsere Liebe" ', 187 (my translation).

[11] The voice-leading implications of Ex. 2.1.2 are discussed on pp. 49–50.

Certainly one of the general ways in which this music gains its vocality is from the perspective in which Brahms sets the voice against the music as a whole. As we have seen, there is a proportional device here whereby the narrative is marked out against the piano introduction and transitions, as if the text were being delivered in quotation marks, proportionally framed, offset, to be contemplated in the musical foreground. This effect is reinforced by the overlap shown in a diagram above whereby the piano 'introduction' locks into the proportional structure a bar earlier at bar 21 than periodic phrasing would lead us to expect: needless to say, this rolls the music forward for us and is an equally effective impetus when used again at bar 41 in anticipation of the first part of the poetic dialogue as the young man finally speaks (Leonard Bernstein gave examples of what he called the 'ready, steady, go' principle in classical music; and although Bernstein received a rather condescending press from theorists, as a kind of archetype of musical phrasing his idea makes perfectly good intuitive sense).[12] The longer transition at bars 68–78 has also been mentioned already, when we noted its proportional fluidity (again, carrying the music forward between the blocks of dialogue) and also, in passing, its pitch-structural function in 'planting' the focal note F sharp that is to dominate the climax of the girl's affirmation: this transition also carries the music from a *forte* dynamic down to the *pianissimo* at which she begins, and through a *ritardando* it ensures a smooth link between the two time signatures (see above). And finally, the transition at bars 94–8 again reasserts the F sharp, this time in its authentic register (as also mentioned) while providing the last 'asymmetrical' background against which the periodic certainty of the love-declaration is set in relief.

One good reason to mention these points of articulation in the song is that we know they were of a kind that Brahms held to be of prime importance. The best evidence of this came from his composition student Gustav Jenner, whom many secondary sources rightly cite as our most reliable authority for certain attitudes of Brahms, who was mostly secretive about his compositions and his experiences as a composer. Jenner was clearly a fine musician himself, as his own compositions testify, as well as being an apparently honest writer. Thus it is often mentioned that Brahms believed the poem must first be absorbed in all possible precision and as a whole (in striking contrast to what Schoenberg said and is believed to have really thought about the essence of setting a text; see Chapter 3,

---

[12] Leonard Bernstein, *The Unanswered Question: Six Talks at Harvard*, Cambridge, Mass., Harvard University Press, 1976.

pp. 62–3). What does not seem to have been discussed by other writers, though, is the question of articulation, despite the fact that Jenner tells us more about this than perhaps any other single feature of the Brahms approach:

I should . . . mark the pauses especially and follow these later when I was working. 'Just imagine to yourself that Lewinsky were reciting this song', he said once as we were discussing a song with almost no pauses; 'here he would certainly stop for a moment'. It is particularly pleasurable to observe the way that Brahms knew how to treat these pauses in his songs, how they are often an echo of what precedes them, often a preparation for what follows ('Von ewiger Liebe'); how here, at times, the rhythm undergoes an artistic development and the accompaniment is raised to a factor that has its own independent influence. He placed great importance on these pauses and their treatment, and they are often, in fact, an unmistakable sign that the composer is an artist who creates with freedom and assurance, not a dilettante groping in the dark, influenced by every chance occurrence. Once the song's structure had been examined from all these angles, there followed a consideration of its individual parts. At those points where language inserts punctuation, the musical phrase has cadences; and just as the poet, in his purposeful constructions, ties his sentences more or less closely together using commas, semicolons, periods, etc., as his external signs, so the musician, similarly, has at his disposal perfect and imperfect cadences in a variety of forms to indicate the greater or lesser degree of coherence of his musical phrases. The importance of the cadences is immediately evident, for it is through them that both the construction and the proportion of the various parts are determined. Thus Brahms, too, focused my particular attention on them.[13]

It is almost coincidental, regarding the argument here, that Jenner does mention our song, since there are after all hundreds of examples in Brahms of his great skill in dramatic articulation, most readily observable in the handling of what Jenner calls the 'pauses' (that is, the breaks in the text); but it is also no accident at all that in his memoir of 1905 Jenner is accounting for music – Brahms's – that remains exemplary of the Lied even a century later and worth contemplating now in its enduring freshness, in the way we have been doing, and in the more subcutaneous ways to follow.

* * *

By subcutaneous I mean that against that backdrop of an informal assimilation of Brahms's song – and some degree of technical explanation that

---

[13] Gustav Jenner, 'Brahms as Man, Teacher, and Artist', in *Brahms and His World*, ed. Walter Frisch, Princeton, Princeton University Press, 1990, 185–204; 197–8. The Lewinsky mentioned is Josef Lewinsky, a famous Viennese actor well known to Brahms: for more information see *Brahms and His World*, 204n.

has not yet, as will be obvious, touched on the 'idea' of this music, on what makes it so melodically unforgettable from one perfectly turned phrase to the next – there are some challenging questions to be answered. Firstly, is the whole 121-bar musical structure really being said to depend for its meaning on *one note* sung nine bars from the end? Does what Schenker called 'distance-hearing' ('*Fernhören*') really operate not only over long spans of music (this is a relatively short one compared with, for example, some of the Beethoven movements analysed by Schenker) but also in revealing such a degree of control over the general by the particular? Secondly, how does Brahms manage to write an entire scenario of this kind – fairly short the poem may be, but it has the rich, tripartite dramatic structure outlined above that in synopsis we could call landscape/question/answer – all in one key? Both questions are, frankly, in search of unity, for there may appear on the surface to be a lack of it in this song, which the first great technical chronicler of Brahms, Edwin Evans Snr, expressed quite strongly: 'The song is cast in three divisions, each having its own separate melody and without any feature of return or other sign of unity to which Brahms was so much attached.'[14] Thirdly, what makes this a song, specifically that kind of music, and not music that, for instance, could be transcribed for instrumental performance without text?[15]

1. In answering the first question, it is tempting to outline a theory of musical structure first conceived by a young man, Heinrich Schenker, in Brahms's old age. Formulated fully in writings through the 1920s and early 1930s (after Schenker's long experience as not only a piano teacher but also one of Europe's finest piano accompanists who regularly played with, for example, the great Russian bass Chaliapin), disseminated among cognoscenti such as Schoenberg (who studied some of Schenker's writings in intense detail, as we know from annotations in his personal library), the great conductor

---

[14] Edwin Evans, *Historical, Descriptive, & Analytical Account of the Entire Works of Johannes Brahms: The Vocal Works*, London, Reeves, 1912, 148. I am not at all convinced that 'Von ewiger Liebe' is any less integrated than is to be found generally in Brahms. At the motivic level, the ubiquitous repeated notes are a sure sign of this (compare the piano opening and the piano introduction to the girl's song, and bearing in mind that both of these repeated-note ideas are sustained in one way and another through their respective sections of the song). Similarly, the reader need only scan the song for melodic 'cells' of a rising or falling stepwise third progression to hear the kind of motivic saturation that Evans correctly attributes to Brahms as characteristic; this is aside from the underlying voice-leading continuities that Evans in the early twentieth century would not have had the theoretical techniques to identify and explain.

[15] Transcribability as a late-Romantic musical criterion is discussed in my essay 'Chamber Music and Piano', in *The Cambridge History of Nineteenth-Century Music*, ed. Jim Samson, Cambridge, Cambridge University Press, 2002, 501–4.

Furtwängler (an avid student of Schenker's book on Beethoven's Ninth Symphony), and many, many other leading practitioners of the early and mid twentieth century, Schenker's theory was then discovered in the world of musical scholarship, criticism and education in the later twentieth century, to be turned into a kind of industry-standard mode of description of the masterpieces of the major-minor tonal period (often referred to, including by Schenker himself, as culminating in Brahms), and to be applied in greater and lesser degrees of adaptation to a good cross-section of music of the twentieth century itself.

The temptation is easily resisted, since music theory is its own specialism with its own history and I am relying on it in this book – all the way from eighteenth-century contrapuntal theory and the nineteenth century's concept of tonal harmony to more recent ideas of how the atonal pitch universe may work – only highly selectively. What one needs to know here about Schenkerian practice is as simple as one might expect from an elegant and comprehensive theory. Music like this, it asserts, has a 'Fundamental Line', which consists of a Primary Melodic Note connected to the closing tonic melody note by stepwise descent, and that Primary Melodic Note is always either the third or fifth degree of the scale of the key of the piece (or, rarely, it may be the eighth degree so that the Fundamental Line descends over the space of an octave from an upper to a lower tonic melody note). Armed with this information and taking it on trust, any reader who cares to study 'Von ewiger Liebe' will see without difficulty that the vocal line does seem to behave in something like this way.

The singer sings 237 notes in this music. Between her lowest and highest notes, in B major only 12 different pitches are available, or in B minor only 14 (since in the minor mode there are two possible choices for the submediant and the leading note), and in the total chromatic between B and F sharp in the higher octave only 20. But the statistics of occurrence are not directly related to musical meaning: if Brahms had taken it into his head to end this song with the sole occurrence of a high E sharp (which does not appear anywhere at all, although it might well have done in various places in the piano accompaniment) it would not be statistically prominent but nevertheless one of the oddest and most conspicuous of notes he had ever written. Looking rather, say, at the final, cadential note of each phrase, notes that are thus of clear contextual significance, we find D (bars 12 and the varied repetition at 32), B (bar 21) and F sharp at the varied repetition, bar 41, F sharp at bars 52 and 60 with B at bar 68 closing the middle section, then F sharp at bar 94 and B at bar 117: not surprisingly, notes only of the triad that represents the tonic of the piece (tonic minor as it happens – there

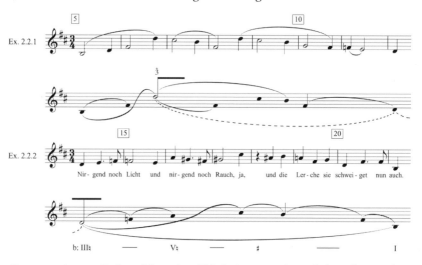

Ex. 2.2.1 and 2.2.2: Brahms, 'Von ewiger Liebe', piano, opening melody, and voice, close of first complete phrase

could have been a D sharp had Brahms's imagination worked differently in this instance).

And if we look instead, as we should, at the musical shapes of what Brahms composed, an even more coherent picture emerges. In Ex. 2.2.1 the opening piano line has been isolated, and the analytical annotations show what nobody is likely to dispute, that D, the third degree of the scale, is the note marking the expressive peak of Brahms's melody. Not only that, but if we were to analyse just the melody in bars 12 to 21 we would want to know where the C sharp in bar 17 comes from, exposed in the higher register as it is: clearly there is a linear connection with D from bar 6, reinforced by the prolongation of D in the lower register. If this seems to be threatening to labour an analytical point, note how Brahms has used the C sharp to yield a piquant catch in the melody (Ex. 2.2.2) where the text '*ja*' injects the voice of the narrator, difficult to translate, but perhaps it is best conveyed as something like 'ah yes', or if it were a less formal kind of script then something like ' – and guess what? – ' might be what is actually said, by the poet, of course; in Brahms's context it becomes a personal bond between *singer* and audience, a taking of us into her confidence. Although there is nothing unusual about this feature, it is a fine little example of the kind of narrative swerve that anchors vocality. Reading the poem to oneself, one somehow hears the poet at that '*ja*' and has to recreate the voice inside the text in whatever way one wishes: the song, however, takes this swerve out of our hands – or minds – and fixes it as part of the illusion of dramatic reality before us, differently rendered by each different singer and from one performance to another; but because of the way Brahms has written this catch into the material of the music, one thing that is not going to happen in any performance is it being glossed over, and this reveals the immense authority of the musical text.

I leave it to the interested reader to listen to the middle section, the young man's part of the dialogue, from this point of view as to the overall sense of a prolonged D, which is entirely unmistakable around bars 47–9, 55–7 and in the last small phrase from bar 61. What the Schenkerian is listening for, however, and anyone with ears to hear, as Brahms would certainly have agreed, is the linear connections of seamless musical invention, and the piano continuation here does complete a picture of the voice-leading that shows a dramatic musical development just at the point where the poem reaches its crisis, a crisis of love threatened and at risk of being ended as fast as it started.

The vocal line has already at its climactic point used one of those leaps of a seventh (F sharp to E in bar 66) that we can easily hear as a virtual stepwise motion, and not least because it is often used in just that way with no special significance.[16] Here, though, one may be permitted to feel that the acutely heightened expressive link from E to D (the young man reminds the girl of that once-in-a-lifetime, instantaneous moment when their love first burst upon them, '*vereiniget sind*') draws the preceding lower F sharp to it, and the piano then asserts this pitch (see Ex. 2.3) in its first ringing appearance of this kind in the piece, 'sung' out in the tenor register, elaborated twice in the quaver neighbouring-note phrase that the piano remembers hearing sung passionately just a little earlier (bars 47 and 55, 'if it grieves you', 'love shall be ended', and also the less literally but nevertheless strongly related figure in bar 63, 'dissolve in the wind', which it transposes up a third now to encircle the resonant, turbulent, decisive fifth degree of the scale). If this is another silly love song, it is nevertheless showing its colours as one of those luxuriously integrated Viennese tonal structures that Schenker went to such pains to explain in all their hierarchical consistency, where each facet of the musical surface is seen to reflect an underlying grand musical

---

[16] There are many well-known cases, for example in Mozart's Clarinet Quintet where he is bumping against the lower range of the instrument and can effortlessly take up a descending line in a higher octave with the added value of expressive upward melodic sevenths. We need look no further than bars 100–1 of 'Von ewiger Liebe' itself, low C sharp to high B, for a similar example, although in Brahms's panorganic structures one hesitates to fail to acknowledge the expressive weight of even such an apparently passing feature, and although in voice-leading terms this is a case where the part is moving between an inner voice (cf. the piano in bar 80) and then its own voice.

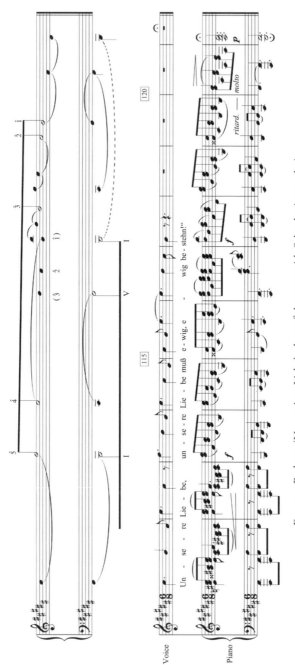

Ex. 2.3: Brahms, 'Von ewiger Liebe', close of the song with Schenkerian analysis

narrative. And it is a particularly interesting case in that the 'goal' of the melodic voice-leading is, as we have seen, emergent rather than a given from the beginning of the music. The unfolding of the structure – if the reader is willing to go along with this metaphorical picture of the music – keeps track with the narrative. It is (how could we doubt it?) F sharp with which now the girl soothingly, wise beyond her years perhaps, driven to certain knowledge by the sheer depth of her emotion, takes up the pitch level offered to her by the soft bell toll of the piano and the voice of the narrator ('Then says the girl'). The rest is history, for it will turn out, in my reading at least, that F sharp will be the Primary Melodic Note at the head of the final stepwise descent to the tonic across bars 113–19 (see Ex. 2.1.2 above), with the particularly integrating feature that the voice and the piano seem to depend on each other for the full expression of the structural 'descent' by step from the dominant note to the tonic.[17] No wonder that the piano sinks in the closing bars precisely from its point of completion of the Fundamental Line (bar 119) in a *molto ritardando* with *diminuendo*, the full intensity of the climactic moment having been spent in the girl's exultant final phrase and the piano's rounding off of the structural descent.

It was asked earlier, somewhat self-provocatively no doubt, whether the whole 121-bar musical structure really can be said to depend for its meaning on *one note* sung nine bars from the end? It may be that such a theatrical kind of question is overplaying what analysis can bring to our understanding and appreciation of a piece of music, although I would note that 'innocent' criticism as opposed to technical analysis seems to involve such heightened evaluation all the time, for example when the redoubtable Henry Colles writes of 'Von ewiger Liebe' that 'the noble words . . . appealed strongly to Brahms, and produced not only a beautiful melody but a magnificent climax in which the eternal nature of pure love is shown'[18] – a somewhat larger claim than that of a delayed Primary Melodic Note. And it is not as if the technical implication of what is specified here about the Fundamental Line had not previously ever been expressed, by implication, equally strongly, as for instance in Sick's understated observation that 'the climax grows

---

[17] The voice does of course descend by step, literally, in bars 115^2–117^1, but I think readers familiar with a voice-leading approach will agree that this is a foreground reflection of the underlying progression where each note of this final descent carries an arpeggio-type melodic prolongation. Presumably one of the reasons why the piano's melodic coda (F sharp – E – D sharp, bars 120–1) is so satisfying and conclusive is that it echoes the emphasized anticipation of the Fundamental Line completion just heard.

[18] Henry Colles, *Brahms*, London, The Bodley Head, 1920, 111.

organically from the musical unfolding through increasing complexity'.[19]
Yet what, it might be asked, if Brahms had written only D sharps in voice
and piano at the top of the texture on the first beat of bar 113? Would
this somehow destroy the meaning of the whole composition? My honest
answer is yes, but with the proviso that it is not a hugely interesting question,
any more than if we asked what would be our dramatic experience if at the
very end of his amazing tragedy King Lear were to say, somewhat to our
astonishment and grossly out of character, 'Ah well, such is life.' Analysis is
not really in the business of saying how things might have been, but how
they are. More to the point then, it is hoped, is the idea that Brahms has
created an integrated and comprehensible imaginary world here, and this
idea will be crucial in addressing the third question about what makes this
song a song.

2. Meanwhile, however, there is the more technical question of how such
a self-evidently opulent structure could be 'all in one key', as it was put
above. Once again it is from Jenner that we can learn highly instructive
poietic information (information, that is, about what goes into a work of
art, regardless of what we think we take from it), which is not only about
Brahms and tonality, a topic on which there is so little contemporaneous
information, but specifically in relation to song composition:

Even in the case of a very long song whose subsidiary phrases were extended and
internally consistent, the principal key always had to be clearly articulated and its
dominance of the secondary keys maintained by means of clear relationship, so
that, so to speak, the sum of all the keys utilized in the piece combined to create an
image of the tonic key in its activity. That precisely the lack of clear identification of
a key, even the tonic, can serve as an excellent means of expression, is in the nature
of the matter. The splendid freedom we sense in Brahms's creative power is rooted
in part in his instinctively sure sense of the unified character of the modulation; and
the saying that it is only by subordinating himself that man can be truly free finds
in him a beautiful confirmation. How often, when listening to songs, particularly
modern songs, must one wonder why a certain song has to end in A-flat major
and find no answer except that it began in A-flat major? Here the composer, who
appears to move so freely in his modulations, has actually become the slave of
an idea whose true meaning he does not seem to grasp. He would be much more
consistent in his arbitrariness if he ended in some other key into which he had been
led just as his text was coming to its conclusion. For a unified modulation does
not in any way preclude the use of even the most distant keys. Quite the contrary,
these keys become distant only by virtue of the fact that another key governs;
this is what gives them their expressive power. They say something different; they

[19] Sick, ' "Unsere Liebe" ', 188.

are like the colors of a painting that contrast with the background color and are simultaneously contained and intensified by it.[20]

There we have a nicely informal documentary statement of the theory of tonality that was being forged by others in great technical detail in the early twentieth century, in particular in the books offering a comprehensive theory of harmony by Schenker and Schoenberg of 1906 and 1911 respectively. 'Von ewiger Liebe' is hardly an example of the kind of extended tonality that Jenner and his teacher had in mind, and as a case from Brahms is in one sense quite strikingly monoharmonic: to put this crudely, much of the song is in the tonic prolonged by the main harmonic supports of that tonic (dominant harmony with supertonic and submediant prolongation between tonics and dominants). In this one sense the tonality doubtless conjures a certain 'folk' style that is also signalled by the brush of modal (dorian) harmony when the flat leading note harmony (A major in B minor) is used as a neighbouring harmony to decorate the tonic, prominently in the opening phrase (bar 3) and several times subsequently in passing. That little folksy feature of the minor-mode sections generates one of the supremely expressive 'classical' figures in the major-mode 'girl' section, when the voice rises over the rocking tonic-dominant piano accompaniment to the so-called 'flat' 7th degree (A natural in B major), prolonged by the 9th (C sharp) approached through a delicate double grace note (bars 84–5, 210–11). I am resisting in all these accounts any kind of 'words cannot describe' approach to such musical effects, which would be curiously self-defeating for the author, let alone the reader, but this use of the 7th in 'Von ewiger Liebe' is in the end something one simply must hear in all its sonic beauty, which is worth saying because it reminds us how much the true impact of song can depend on what the performer brings to it for us, here with a certain intonation (how flat is a flat 7th?). The ear, the ordinary listener's ear, can pick up the singer's take on this to the tiniest fraction of a semitone, just a few barely measurable cents in terms of the vibrational 'frequency' of the pitch used, and with a certain articulation of the tiny grace notes up to the 9th that, similarly, has its own magical microrange of intonation. One could even venture some conceit about Brahms thus first presenting and then subsequently 'domesticating' a folk element within the same compositional arena: there would be some truth in that, although it could well be to labour a point.[21]

---

[20] Jenner, 'Brahms as Man', 189–90.

[21] There are two good reasons for not labouring the point. Firstly, Brahms does often use the modal inflection of the 7th in large canvases in elaborate ways, as for example in the German Requiem. Secondly, when he wants to make a big feature of the interplay between the folk and the classical, it

Aside from that one sense of continuity, however, there are two ways in which the song is sustained here while being not only 'all in one key', but firmly grounded in that key without 'tonicized' harmonic steps – which is how Schenkerian terminology refers to nontonic key areas in order to represent their status as always related to the background tonic of the piece – or in other words, without modulations. Firstly, in the overall structure there is as we have seen a shift in mode from minor (verses 1–3) to major (verses (4–5). The lullaby effect of the girl's speech (the cliché 'gently rocking' suits it so well) is all the more etched for being in a sudden major mode. The kind of organic seed, often so hidden as to go unnoticed except on very close inspection, that composers typically plant for later flowerings in a work is to be found in the first 78 bars, for one fleeting modal shift has already occurred, when III (D major) is turned to minor in bars 10–11 (and the D minor in itself is important, as will be explained shortly). Some may also find the move from minor V (F sharp minor) to the harmonic dominant, F sharp major, in bars 16–18 a precedent for modal change, a tiny model of it, and especially perhaps in that the chromatic alteration added by the $I^{\#}$– IV in bar 19 produces closely written inflections from A to its sharp version, to the natural, and back to the sharp across a mere five bars. In the passages preceding the girl's speech, however, bars 45–78, there is no overt or covert hint of anything but the minor mode: at the level of finest detail, perhaps the two dominant-function bars at 52 and 60 invite comment in that there is no A sharp sounded at all (so do we really hear these bars as minor V, and if so, is not such an unusual connection to the tonic an invitation to sense 'chromaticism', thus the potential for modal change at work?); and equally one may speculate whether after the sustained diatonicism of the preceding thirty bars the leading notes immediately before the girl's entry, where E sharp moves to F sharp in the bass (bars 77–8) and B predictably drops to A sharp (bars 78–9), ask the unconscious ear whether D is going to lead to D sharp? Still it can be said, for all such scrupulous analysis of technical implications anticipating it, that the B major comes as a new breath, an operatic veering from one character to another who has an entirely different perspective to offer.

can be in cases of extensively sustained compositional virtuosity, of which the finale of the G minor Piano Quartet, Op. 25, is one example, and the final of the Violin Concerto another that is very much more veiled, although because of the general popularity of the work much more frequently cited. Nevertheless, we can speculate that the charm to be found in the flat 7th (and in the 9th) were on Brahms's mind when he borrowed this melodic idea from his earlier unpublished bridal chorus; see above, note 7.

The other way in which the music is sustained here is more local, but crucial for all that, since it concerns the structural type of the first and second (repeated) verse prior to the overheard drama. Although the generalization was made earlier that much of the song is in the tonic prolonged by the main harmonic supports of that tonic, the harmonic prolongation in the first verse is nevertheless rather advanced, and certainly in music that has the air of a folksong. The structural type is an everyday mediant prolongation, but in particular and unusually a minor mediant prolongation in a minor key: thus the music moves between tonic (B) and dominant (F sharp) through D minor, which is a remote harmony in the sense, for instance, that its third degree, F, cancels the fifth degree of the tonic B, F sharp. It has an eerie effect at bars 14–17 the first time (perhaps especially so in harness with the spooky words, 'und nirgend noch Rauch' as the voice rises to a dissonant sequence that is shaped in such a way as to highlight the tritone D to G sharp – one possible technical result of the strange transposition from a minor triad to a minor triad four semitones higher); no doubt we accept the second sounding of this in bars 34–7 according to the aesthetic convention that strophic repetition does not necessarily, or often, rehearse the impact of the initial idea, or, if you prefer, the willow bushes can be taken to be part of the threatening landscape and worth a second small shudder.[22] The progression has enormous structural potential, not to be realized in this song. We can appreciate that potential directly from Brahms's B minor Rhapsody, Op. 79, No. 1 of 1878, where not only is this precise model of i-iii-v (i.e., minor triads) in B used in the opening section, but the entire first 'A' section of this mighty 'A-B-A' construction (incidentally, with a middle, 'B' section in B major) prolongs the i-iii-v structural type, its lyrical, folksong-like second theme, after the stormy (Hungarian?) opening, being in a gliding D minor before the virtuosic tonicization of the dominant F sharp leads to the varied reprise in B.

What this tells us is something about the contained, latent, undeveloped harmonic power of the opening verses of 'Von ewiger Liebe': and this is

---

[22] Across the cultures the willow has had as many benign symbolic 'meanings' as threatening ones: see for example Hans Biedermann, *Knaurs Lexikon der Symbole*, Munich, Droemer Knaur, 1989, 476–7. But within German poetry it tends to carry the latter; a well-known example is in Goethe's poem 'Der Erlkönig' ('The Erlking'), which Brahms certainly knew, if only from Schubert's famous setting of 1815, with its line 'The old willows look so grey', which is the last thing the father says in this gruesome poem, carrying his infant son home only to find him dead on arrival. On the other hand, Kalbeck calls the willow in 'Von ewiger Liebe' a 'haven' of love (which is one way to translate Kalbeck's poetic word '*Asyl*' that can also denote much the same as the English word 'asylum' as to circumscribed safety). See Kalbeck, *Johannes Brahms*, 131. I have not found anywhere in Kalbeck where he gives a reason for this interpretation of the poem's willow bushes.

how, from one point of view, another far-from-silly love song can be all in one key.

3. To answer the question 'what makes this song a song?' is on the one hand in danger of stating the obvious, which may have its place sometimes, but is also what often gives musical discourse and would-be music analysis in particular a bad name. For example, in Schenkerian analysis, of which there is an oblique and very cursory introduction above for those who may appreciate it or need to be reminded, it is unfortunately quite common to see lengthy verbal descriptions of analytical features that ought to be, and very often are, obvious and better assimilated from a graphic, voice-leading representation of the music. One strong drive in Schenker's thinking was to replace verbal approximation with graphic precision, so that, for instance, a contrapuntal figure (say, a voice exchange) underlying a more elaborate surface prolongation in the music can simply be 'seen' by the literate musician (not unlike the way in which if someone holds up three fingers we 'see' instantly that there are three without counting); a really accurate verbal description of the same figure and of its relationship to the musical surface could take hundreds, thousands of words, at the end of which one would be attempting in any case some kind of metaphorical assimilation of the reading that makes sense to the musical intuition. It is precisely in the light of this that the graphic, bass-line reading of Copland's 'Going to Heaven' in Chapter 5 is more or less presented as is, free from the very many pages that could easily be written about it. It is worth mentioning that one of the common benefits perceived by those who enjoy Schenker-graphs is the freedom of interpretation they give to the reader; one of the ironies of musicological debate is that Schenkerian work is sometimes discussed as being authoritarian, telling the listener how to hear, when it merely intends to impart what is happening in the music, make of it what you will – the interpretations of Brahms's song offered above are in the spirit of just that idea.

Aside from being in danger of stating the obvious, answering the question of what is songful about 'Von ewiger Liebe' is on the other hand in danger of shooting for the moon, just as it would be to ask what is 'instru-mental' about a Beethoven string quartet. We can, for sure, point to certain characteristics of this composition that mark it out as what it is: that was largely the purpose of our detailed discussions above. And it does seem to be incontestable that 'Von ewiger Liebe' involves periodicities in the vocal line, deliberately or at least unmistakably foregrounded by the asymmetrical phrasing at turning points in the accompaniment, and these periodicities reflect the balladesque, the folksong, as well as reflecting the stylized metre and rhyming of the text itself with its regular line-lengths and transparent sound-couplings, all of which are far removed – as is one of the pleasures of stylized poetry – from everyday narration and speech. It also involves a high degree of redundancy in that each musical 'verse' (beginning at lines 1, 9 and 15) is repeated, albeit in slightly or significantly varied form (lines 4, 11 + 13 and 19 respectively), and if one encounters such a highly repetitive form in even an unpretentious instrumental piece (maybe a waltz or a polka), it is likely to be called 'songlike' in recognition of the textually motivated formal archetype. We have also observed that the harmonic design of the music is, although sharply etched (mainly in the light of the mediant minor prolongation in the opening verses), nevertheless highly restricted, to the extent that a purely instrumental version of this music might well give rise to a feeling of harmonic uneventfulness, of a deliberate compositional restraint for some unknown reason (a reason that, in the song itself, the vivid, dense story provides from beginning to end in its uninterrupted unfolding). Additionally, there are no rests in this music, literally, although there are profoundly implicative 'pauses' (Jenner's word taken from Brahms's teaching; see p. 43) that are certainly at the heart of one dimension of the vocality of the song.

Whether we can ever get to the essence, the quiddity, of an object such as 'Von ewiger Liebe' must remain doubtful. What one person hears, textually, as a heartrending story of undying love, another may experience as cloying sentimentality. And one person's heightened musical Romanticism, with its aperiodic phrasing and its richly implicative mediant harmony, for example, may be another's major-minor, common-practice period, post-Classical string of musical clichés. It is entirely possible that the story is true of Wagner being bored to the point of nodding off while listening, rather unwillingly one imagines, to Brahms playing his Handel Variations, and not without reason in that the neo-Baroque taste of the 1850s being cultivated by the Mendelssohn/Schumann circle including the young Brahms was not likely to be to everyone's taste; even if purely instrumental music could be tolerated and appreciated as a restricted but occasionally worthwhile medium, with memories of Liszt and Chopin as composer-performers ringing in their ears, this New German seriousness (even in Brahms's early, exuberant, partly programmatic piano sonatas) could understandably need to be an acquired taste for Wagner and his adherents. Nevertheless, within the circles, including those today, where a taste for Brahms's aesthetic is still alive – and he does count as one of the most popular, frequently heard 'geniuses' of classical music – 'Von ewiger Liebe' has a special place as a supreme expression of replete vocality.

Perhaps one of its special features to be mentioned in closing is that it is a true representative of the class of accompanied solo song. Very often in the Romantic Lied the accompaniment has, as we discuss in various places in this book, its own 'voice', more often than not taking on some of the dramatic personification of action or sentiments in the text: hence the currently fashionable phrase 'the voice of the piano' (or the voice of the orchestra in a work such as 'Premonition' discussed in Chapter 3). This can yield some of the most complex and intriguing musical interrelationships requiring the most sensitive analysis of the resultant double-narratives and their contrasts and complementarities. I would suggest, though, that in 'Von ewiger Liebe' Brahms has avoided such potential complications in favour of a narrative unity where the piano works always *with* the voice, responding, enhancing, anticipating perhaps (see, for example, the subtle crescendo in bar 44 at the 'edit' between the opening scene and the young man's speech), and embracing it in the all-important melodic closure. If I have more or less avoided the temptation to rhapsodize about the structural fusion of voice and piano in the very fabric of the music as a representation of the coming together of our unnamed stars in their eternal love, nevertheless it is there for those who can agree.

CHAPTER 3

Boundless opulence: postscripts on
Schoenberg's premonition

If much of the music discussed in this book can be considered either popular or at least familiar and accessible, the same may not be quite true
of Schoenberg's orchestral song 'Premonition', Op. 22, No. 4, or indeed
music of Kurtág and Berberian to be discussed in Chapter 4. Although
Op. 22 is mentioned often enough in the Schoenberg literature, this is not
a work that is frequently performed or that has been recorded by many
different artists. There is something difficult about the music; as has been
perfectly obvious for nearly a century, there is something 'difficult' about
Schoenberg's music anyway.

The encouraging title of this chapter, 'Boundless opulence', is a translated phrase taken from Alban Berg's apparently discouraging essay, to go
by its famous title at least, 'Why is Schoenberg's Music So Hard to Understand?'.[1] Although that issue, of the nature of the difficulty of understanding
Schoenberg's music, is not the main issue in this chapter, there will be some
attempt to deal with it obliquely; this will not be by avoiding it, but in a
sense by complicating it (as a by-product rather than an intention) by asking what 'difficulty' may mean in the context of vocality. It is not so much a
question of whether Schoenberg's music for voice and instruments is inherently more difficult than his purely instrumental music, or his *a cappella*
vocal music, one choice item of which will be contemplated more briefly
in Chapter 4; rather the question is whether 'difficulty' is a useful paradigm
for musical thinking, paying all due respect to Berg's rhetorical purposes
in foregrounding what appears on the face of it to be a negative – or at
least hardly uplifting – approach to assimilating avowedly 'modernistic'
music.

---

[1] Alban Berg, 'Why is Schoenberg's Music So Hard to Understand?', in *Contemporary Composers on
Contemporary Music*, ed. E. Schwartz and B. Childs, New York, Da Capo Press, 1967, 59–71; 69. This
translation first appeared in *The Music Review*, 13/2, May 1952, 187–96. It was originally published
by Berg as 'Warum ist Schönbergs Musik so schwer verständlich?', in *Musikblätter des Anbruchs*, 8/8,
August/September 1924, 329–41.

It needs to be said almost at the outset that this music, Schoenberg's Op. 22, No. 4, is not being exhibited as a special case of challenge to musical understanding. Far from it. True, in Schoenberg's music over some five decades there appeared a tendency towards what has been called artificiality or contrivance – in his shoe-horning of twelve-note technique into conventional forms, for example, especially in the notoriously unforgiving Wind Quintet, Op. 26, or in his squeezing out of twelve-note technique some uncomfortable, discomforting tonal resolution (E flat major, the key of Beethoven's *Eroica* Symphony) in the 'Ode to Napoleon', Op. 42. It is thought likely by specialists in Schoenberg biography that he never heard his Four Orchestral Songs in performance, remarkable though we now find this of a piece that has come to be regarded as a hallmark of expressionist imaginative force, to judge from its typical characterization in the musicological literature. And it might be said without undue generalization that compositional 'artificiality' and 'contrivance' were never *less* apparent in Schoenberg than in his compositions of roughly the second decade of the twentieth century, when he was in his late thirties and early forties. Those in whom listening to 'Premonition' evokes afterthoughts about freshness, immediacy, inspiration and so on have surely come close to what the composer wanted and to what are the most important truths to be found in the music. That said, there is undeniably a less than welcoming aura to the Op. 22 songs, and not least to 'Premonition', a sense, perhaps an unavoidable sense, that although there is nothing of itself wrong with the song – in its beauty, craftsmanship, maturity, its 'thought-out' quality – it is nevertheless somehow to be approached with caution. It is not 'easy listening'. One can even say, if somewhat extravagantly, that it seems a little dangerous, a little toxic. It was shortly before this time that Schoenberg had also been painting a great deal, especially around 1912 under the influence of Kandinsky (see p. 63), including among many self-portraits a lot of heads, two of which the art critic David Sylvester, writing originally in 1960, mentioned as 'haunting images, weird and *strained*'.[2]

And from the outset, too, we have to think about the fact that this is music with a text:[3]

---

[2] David Sylvester, *About Modern Art: Critical Essays 1948–97*, London, Pimlico, 1997, 77 (my emphasis).
[3] Rilke's 1902 poem in Roman print here has been interspersed with my literal translation enabling the German words to be understood more or less one-by-one. The most frequently encountered and much-anthologized translation is that by Robert Bly: it has a certain poetic intent, for instance with its title 'Sense of Something Coming' (rather than 'Premonition') and a certain freedom in translation (for example, by referring in line 1 to a 'flag in the center of open space') that has its merits, but it is not and is not intended to be, of course, a simulacrum of what Schoenberg was 'reading' in the German original.

Vorgefühl (Premonition)

Ich bin wie eine Fahne von Fernen umgeben.
I am like a flag by distances surrounded
Ich ahne die Winde, die kommen, und muss sie leben,
I sense the winds that come and must endure them
während die Dinge unten sich noch nicht rühren:
while the things below still do not move
die Türen schließen noch sanft, und in den Kaminen ist Stille;
the doors close still softly, and in the chimneys there's silence
die Fenster zittern noch nicht, und der Staub ist noch schwer.
the windows do not rattle yet, and the dust is still heavy
Da weiß ich die Stürme schon und bin erregt wie das Meer.
this is for me the storms already and I'm aroused like the sea
Und breite mich aus und falle in mich hinein
and spread myself out and fold into myself
und werfe mich ab und bin ganz allein
and throw myself down and am quite alone
in dem großen Sturm.
in the mighty storm   Rilke (1902)

On the one hand, the text itself may be taken for granted, as it were, as the centre of attention in our placing and seizing of this work. Paul Banks, for one, quotes Rilke's poem with the comment that 'many of the most powerful and impressive creations of Viennese art in the period leading to 1914 articulated a sense of foreboding and uncertainty . . . Rilke's vision in 1902 was prophetic, Schoenberg's setting of the text in 1916 . . . a grim product of hindsight'.[4] Without for a moment criticizing Banks, it needs to be borne in mind that he is discussing what he calls a 'product', albeit a piece of music, as if it *were* the text, almost as if the song amounted in sum to nothing more than the text had to offer in the first place, which surely cannot be the case in practice, even regardless of the aesthetic principle that it *ought* not to be the case. Similarly, in an essay on Op. 22 in a publication devoted to music-analytical perspectives on Schoenberg's work, Wolfgang Ruf points to the words here, to the dramatic assertions of confidence in his destiny to which Schoenberg allies himself through his chosen text, after a particularly difficult period in his continually difficult personal life.[5] So we see called in evidence, in these emblematic citations, Schoenberg the commentator on the one hand, Schoenberg the confessor on the other hand; not Schoenberg the composer.

[4] Paul Banks, 'Fin-de-siècle Vienna: Politics and Modernism', in *Man & Music: The Late Romantic Era from the Mid-19th Century to World War I*, ed. Jim Samson, London, Macmillan, 1991, 362–88, 384.
[5] Wolfgang Ruf, '*Vier Lieder für Gesang und Orchester*, Op. 22', in *Arnold Schönberg: Interpretationen seiner Werke*, ed. Gerold Gruber, Laaber, Laaber-Verlag, 2002, I, 321–32; 323.

That kind of reductive extreme in writing about music is hard to avoid, and is nothing more than a musical case of the feature we always have to take in our stride in reading history in general, history that can never say everything, and that certainly cannot say everything all at once. Being hard to avoid, however, does not stop the reductive extreme from being a strong shaping force in what we are led to think. The converse, reducing the work to its purely musical substance, is equally extreme potentially, and, as was discussed in Chapter 1, there is always the tendency towards taking a transvocal approach to song in its various forms, towards marginalizing music-and-text realities that are hard to assimilate, other than instinctively perhaps. Transvocality of that kind is precisely Nicholas Cook's stance when he mentions Op. 22 – symbolically, to be fair, and in the interests of building what is undoubtedly his interesting slant on musical experience – as a veritable totem of modernistic complexity and inaccessibility in the struggle to 'imagine' music: 'reading the score in a library', he tells us, and 'without a piano at hand and unable to sing out loud . . . I strain to grasp the sound of Schoenberg's Four Orchestral Songs'.[6] Cook is permitted – anyone would agree – to discuss 'sound' as a salient feature of a piece of music, but to take him at his word here would be to assume that Schoenberg's adoption of Rilke's text, and the text's transformed appearance as part of a piece of music, does not succeed in leading us to grasp the 'sound' of the music, or even in ameliorating the *difficulty* presented by the sound of this music. Schoenberg does not really – Cook is saying, at least for his own part – make these words sing, or not without one being able to sing or play the music, which would massively exclude the wider audience's appreciation that Schoenberg craved from compositional cradle to grave. Although it is common sense to acknowledge that some musical scores, and especially those composed since the beginning of the last century, are hard to 'imagine' in the abstract, in the inner ear, nevertheless it says something about the habits of musical historiography that one may wittingly, no doubt even carefully, select a *song* as an example of such musical difficulty: it says something a little disquieting perhaps about the habits of musicologists, about their assumptions when confronted with the suppressible – possibly *re*pressed? – realities of a perceived musical object; while on the positive side it says something, too, about the ease with which we can assimilate words and music into our general thinking about the musical object.

In one sense that easy assimilation is going to appear now, because in Berg's fascinating essay 'Why is Schoenberg's Music So Hard to

---

[6] Nicholas Cook, *Music, Imagination, and Culture*, Oxford, Clarendon Press, 1990, 96.

Understand?', which will unfold in this encounter with 'Premonition', the music Berg used for illustration was not vocal, but Schoenberg's First String Quartet. This cannot be helped. It is no surprise that Berg did not complicate the picture in his frank and clear attempt to clarify the apparently abstruse world of Schoenberg's melody and harmony, tempted though he may well have been to illustrate from the words-and-music Schoenberg of the third and fourth movements of the Second String Quartet, for example, compositions that are milestones not only in being vocal at all (the 'vocal' string quartet was a *generic* modernism for early twentieth-century chamber music) but also in the fourth, final movement for being among the first overtly 'atonal' compositions (modernism of the very musical *language*).[7] Berg selected music by Schoenberg that although undoubtedly modernistic – or else Berg would not be discussing it in such a context – nevertheless is in a mainstream genre hallowed since Haydn, Mozart and Beethoven, music that has a key signature, that begins with a clearly articulated 'tune', and that bears various other hallmarks of what might be called musical normality. This, too, cannot be helped: 'normal', instrumental music would be a dubious model for guidance through a 'toxic' atonal song were it not for the fact that Berg writes with massive authority, as one of Schoenberg's two closest and most gifted pupils along with Webern, and as a composer with a growing international reputation who was wooing audiences with a repertoire that remained small even by the end of his life in 1935, but that had begun to include what were already well recognized publicly as the enduring favourites of the classical repertoire that nearly all were to become – the Piano Sonata, for instance, the Lyric Suite for string quartet, the opera *Wozzeck*, the Violin Concerto. Berg's authority also stems from the very authenticity of his question, not least in its echo of a little essay by Schoenberg from 1913 called 'Why New Melodies are Difficult to Understand':[8] as Janet Schmalfeldt rightly shows, even if Schoenberg's original essay is relatively short on content, it is one origin of ideas that were to preoccupy him in his theoretical writings for decades[9] – and even though, as indicated in Chapter 1, there is no golden key in them to word/music issues.

---

[7] Berg argues that what was true of Schoenberg's tonal compositions simply must have been true of his subsequent atonal ones *a fortiori*. See ibid., 69.

[8] First published in translation in Bryan Simms, 'New Documents in the Schoenberg-Schenker Polemic', in *Perspectives of New Music*, 16/1, 1977, 115–16. Schoenberg's original essay was published by Universal Edition in *Die Konzertwoche*, and the manuscript is in the Arnold Schoenberg Archive, known as 'Berlin Südende 10/X.1913'.

[9] Janet Schmalfeldt, 'Berg's Path to Atonality', in *Alban Berg: Historical and Analytical Perspectives*, ed. D. Gable and R. Morgan, Oxford, Clarendon, 1990, 79–109.

In the absence of an established sense of critical languages in contemporary music theory to help us discuss and understand relatively modern 'music and text', a certain neologistic urge may be permitted, and the term vocality discussed in the Introduction and introduced in Chapter 1 responds to that urge. It refers, to revisit its semantic aura in this new context, to those qualities of music and text that enable one to identify it as articulating narrative, mood, the times of tenses, associations, grammatical tropes such as the interrogative, visual images, persons and landscapes, the mundane and the divine. Vocality concerns everything that a replete analysis of music and text ought to explain, and ought not to neglect. By 'transvocal', on the other hand, we have been referring to analytical discoveries concerning purely the domain of musical structure, and this kind of discovery may well render a song indistinguishable from a piece of absolute music, as with Schenker's famous, or notorious, analysis of the second song from Schumann's *Dichterliebe* – and even though I cannot agree with Joseph Kerman's attempt to minimize the hermeneutical potential of that analysis (see p. 32). Now, it has to be acknowledged that according to the institutional criteria of what counts as theory and analysis within systematic musicology, the idea of focusing on vocality as I have described it may seem to be quixotically overambitious, if we expect something to emerge that is like a map of a song, or a Schenkerian chart, or a picture akin to a neo-Riemannian tone-network, or even a sort of table of contents more akin to a traditional formal analysis of autonomous musical structure. But that is not what I expect to emerge. On the contrary, the vocality of a piece of music will always give rise to networks of interpretations, of implications, of inflection and of nuance, and all of them, of course, structurally ambivalent because of the divergences among musical and verbal structures: this was the hoped-for quarry, after all, of the investigation of 'Von ewiger Liebe' in Chapter 2. What will anchor this approach, however, in an ideal world at least, is the evidence; so long as we never lose a sense of the immanence of the work, the 'plot' of the analysis will be guaranteed.[10]

We know that Schoenberg believed a text could, and perhaps usually should, inspire a composer all at once. His claim to have understood Schubert's songs without attending to the words and without being aware of their meaning, let alone their images and tone, was possibly entirely serious

---

[10] A brief discussion of the importance of the idea of 'plot' in music analysis can be found in Jean-Jacques Nattiez's *Music and Discourse: Toward a Semiology of Music*, Princeton, Princeton Univerity Press, 1990, 176–7.

despite any suspicion that he was at least exaggerating if not fabricating his musical experiences. The claim certainly has been taken seriously and often literally among the generations who have been fascinated by his essay 'The Relationship to the Text', in which it appeared.[11] And to Schoenberg, writing in the heady early days of psychoanalysis, under the spell of Kandinsky writing at the same time about the theory of the spiritual in art, and indeed under the spell of Kandinsky's practice on canvas of figurative essentialism based on 'inner necessity',[12] the idea of capturing a contemporary poem in a concentrated but nonspecific essence offered the promise of a close intersection between compositional intention and esthesic response. In other words, that was the kind of response to text that would make Schoenberg's music easier to understand, not harder. For this reason I set no great store by specific depictions in the song, the billowing flag mentioned in Rilke's poem, the restless sea, the mighty storm brewing: it does not take worthwhile critical interpretation to find music/text correspondences at that level if one wants to. The proliferation of Schoenberg's song, however, takes a great deal of assimilation, and I need not dwell on its zeitgeist credentials, ranging as they do, when it comes to extremes of compression, from Wagnerian 'music drama' in Strauss's *Salome* (1905) – which has often been noted as the shortest, most concentrated masterpiece of that genre – to orchestral song in the work of his own pupil, that is, in Berg's *Altenberg Lieder* (1912).

The pitch in Schoenberg's song, for instance, is self-evidently recycling the total chromatic, with referential pitches, especially E flat, and in terms of tonality with the kind of highly occluded reference typical of this period to a potential key, D, which was one of Schoenberg's most common keys, or at least one of his most common focal pitches spanning a movement or work (see also p. 77). This chromatic proliferation, as a vehicle for conveying the threatening uncertainty at the centre of Rilke's poem, is ideal for Schoenberg's kind of compositional scenario – it could have been the very opposite kind of compositional scenario, one in which the ordered, the comfortable, the secure were the aesthetic currency, for which atonal composition was never likely to be suitable, then as nowadays.

Similarly, Schoenberg's rhythms, too, proliferate, and this in an immediately perceptible way, as the ear is tugged up and down through a web

---

[11] Arnold Schoenberg, 'The Relationship to the Text', in *Style and Idea: Selected Writings of Arnold Schoenberg*, London, Faber, 1975, 141–5.

[12] Wassily Kandinsky, 'On the Question of Form', in *The 'Blaue Reiter' Almanac*, ed. Wassily Kandinsky and Franz Marc, New York, Viking Press, 1974, 147–87, 153.

of fine distinctions between fast-moving, duple and triple, often synco-
pated rhythmic figures. If the text were about jewels, as in No. 10 of *Pierrot
lunaire* in which Schoenberg expressed such satisfaction at his depiction,[13]
or if it were a depiction of the infinite starry night sky as at the end of
Verklärte Nacht, which was another of his favourite passages, then the obvious correspondences could pass almost without comment. Here, though,
we have to accept, I believe, that proliferation is Schoenberg's interpretation
of Rilke's premonition. One could imagine an entirely different, austere,
monochrome approach.

However, the locus of proliferation in the vocality of this song may not
be all that it seems, and here the compositional genesis of 'Premonition' is
suggestive. It has been shown from study of the ink overlay in the composer's
holograph that he wrote the orchestral introduction first, not surprisingly
perhaps, then the vocal part, then the accompaniment, something at which
one is hardly entitled to experience much sense of surprise either, in view
of Schoenberg's typical working methods such as we understand them.[14] It
is worth bearing in mind that from the opening of Op. 22 Schoenberg has
imprinted the transcendence of the melodic in his field of values; of all the
possible ways in which he could have initiated this journey through four
heady, earnest, highly personal poems about fundamentals of the human
condition – loss, loneliness, anxiety seem to me the underlying themes – it
is plain melody, in the remarkable sonority of six clarinets, with which the
opening song, 'Seraphita', is initiated (see Ex. 3.1).

Vocality, in other words, is the order of the day well before the voice is even
heard in Op. 22. Now the apparent history of the genesis of 'Premonition'
may not prove anything, but it is strongly suggestive of the idea that the
voice in the fourth song is an integral setting of Rilke's poem. Maybe this
is even what Cook had in mind unconsciously with his sense of needing
to sing out loud when looking at the score of Op. 22 in order to begin to
try to imagine it in 'reality'. When we hear of the motionless calm of the
world below at bars 8–9 of 'Premonition', this I believe is what the voice
represents at that stage of the narrative. The voice is the present tense, as it
were, sensing, enduring and observing. The future tense is thus I suppose
what swirls around the voice in the orchestra. At the level of fine detail,

[13] Jonathan Dunsby, *Schoenberg: Pierrot lunaire*, Cambridge, Cambridge University Press, 1992, 18.
[14] Jonathan Dunsby, 'Schoenberg's Premonition, Op. 22, No. 4, in Retrospect', in *Journal of the Arnold
Schoenberg Institute*, 1/3, 1977, 137–49. Among other specialist literature I refer the reader in particular
to Steven Cahn's 'Variations in Manifold Time: Historical Consciousness in the Music and Writings
of Arnold Schoenberg', PhD dissertation, State University of New York, Stony Brook, 1996; and
Jack Boss's 'Schoenberg's Op. 22 Radio Talk and Developing Variation in Atonal Music', in *Music
Theory Spectrum*, 14/2, Fall 1992, 125–49.

Ex. 3.1: Schoenberg, Four Orchestral Songs, Op. 22, No. 1, 'Seraphita', opening

this is a remarkable process. Already in the poem itself there is a marker of something unusual, since Rilke has the flag referring firstly, assonantly, to surrounding space or distance, but using in German the plural, '*Fernen*', 'distances', of a word almost always read, heard, expected in the singular. Schoenberg has the voice suspended on a G sharp, instructed to sing it with head-tone, so the linguistic marker is well enshrined in the devices of song here; but the instruments provide the perspective on these mysterious 'distances' with E–D sharp on cor anglais and clarinet, which I value most for its shaft of expressive moment, yet which, as Ex. 3.2 shows clinically in

pitch-class representation of bars 1–2:

```
                                          7 -------

        8                    11| -----2   4 -------

        4                     6 | -----3

                                          8  9

        2 5 1 3         | 0 -------- 10 1

                          9 --------  5  9
```

Ex. 3.2: Schoenberg, Four Orchestral Songs, Op. 22, No. 4, 'Premonition', opening and vocal continuation

a pitch-class representation of the opening two bars of the orchestral music, takes up a pitch reference from the opening – these pitches are designated as '4' for E and '3' for D sharp in bar 5^{2-3} of the score, marked in boxes: also, of course, D sharp (pc 3) is the voice's fleeting opening note, and pcs 3 and 4 are the boundary pitches of the voice's first bar before the stasis on G sharp for '*Fernen*'. Similarly, with slightly more complexity, at least in how best to explain it (as the reader who has access to the orchestral score will be able to check), the rhyme word across bars 7–8 at the end of the voice's second line, '*leben*', marked out rhythmically as a musical 'rhyme' with '*Fernen*' in bar 5, induces a memory in the orchestra (in the anacrusis to bar 8 in low woodwind and cellos and the figure of a double anapaest it inaugurates) of the stark, unmissable cello idea from the opening – both of these being, admittedly, fleeting (and in the case of the anacrusis barely perceived) musical moments.

Perhaps the most striking of all such recurrences in this song is the clarinet's *Hauptstimme* anticipation, in bars 13–14, of the vocal line in bar 18, with its repeated sounding of the note G, prolonged by its chromatic upper neighbouring note A flat (Ex. 3.3).

Not only is this of local significance, as the voice picks up on an association, plucking a revenant[15] from the orchestra as she contemplates her disturbed present condition, contrasted with the quiet, unsuspecting world around her, and profoundly self-absorbed and anxious; but it also reinforces the menacing meaning of the opening melodic figure in the orchestra – G sharp (enharmonically, A flat) to G an octave higher via B and D – and anticipates the vocal climax at bar 24, *fortissimo* and strongly reinforced in the orchestra, for the final word 'storm' (see Ex. 3.4).

I wrote of 'proliferation in the vocality of this song', which I have been considering in the rather technical analytical comments just made, and considering them from an essentially poietic viewpoint. Not only would the composer undoubtedly subscribe to such analysis, but in Schoenberg's case one can imagine a certain steely, formalist glint in his eye, for these are just the kinds of musical relationship that we know from his extensive theoretical writings he placed at a premium in the interplay between compositional intention and accultured perception – the perception, that is,

[15] Revenants – entities that haunt, that return – are discussed in a musical context in Chapter 12, 'Ghost Stories: Cultural Memory, Mourning, and the Myth of Originality', of Lawrence Kramer's *Musical Meaning: Toward a Critical History*, Berkeley, University of California Press, 2002, 258–87.

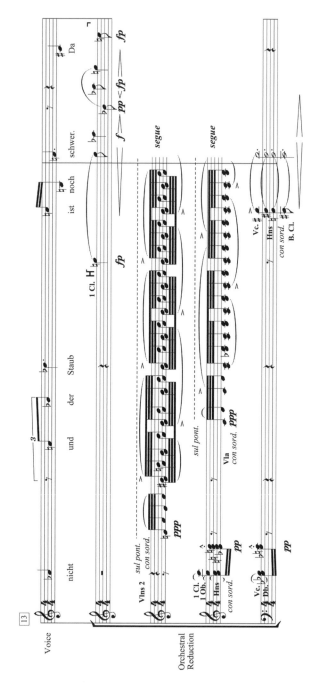

Ex. 3.3: Schoenberg, Four Orchestral Songs, Op. 22, No. 4, 'Premonition', bars 13–14

Ex. 3.4: Schoenberg, Four Orchestral Songs, Op. 22, No. 4, 'Premonition', voice, bars 17–24

not of some supposedly 'naïve' listener,[16] but of an audience that has (to put it informally) some idea of what it is paying for. This proliferation of vocality is not necessarily a preserve of the composer, however, as Carolyn Abbate has argued very interestingly, above all in her book *Unsung Voices*. She offers a long and subtle argument, but I think it does her no disservice to highlight here one of her early conclusions, forming a premise to which I subscribe without hesitation:

> As a consequence of the inherently live and performed existence of music, its own voices are stubborn, insisting upon their privilege. They manifest themselves, in my interpretations, as different *kinds* or modes of music that inhabit a single work. They are not uncovered by analyses that assume all music in a given work is stylistically or technically identical, originating from a single source in 'the Composer'.[17]

Why this is so important a point is that, firstly, it respects the inherent complexity of the artistic object, when so often and wrongly criticism in general, and music analysis in particular, assume that the shifting episte-mological sands of meaning lie in the subject rather than, as is also the case and often more significantly the case, in the object; and secondly, it does apply to music of many kinds, even if Abbate herself is introducing here studies of some of the most interesting cases in opera.[18]

---

[16] The extent to which the naïve or 'ordinary' listener may usefully determine modes of music-analytical discourse is discussed briefly and from one important perspective in Chapter 5, 'The British Context: Tovey', of Jonathan Dunsby and Arnold Whittall, *Music Analysis in Theory and Practice*, London, Faber, 1988, 62–73.

[17] Carolyn Abbate, *Unsung Voices: Opera and Musical Narrative in the Nineteenth Century*, Princeton, Princeton University Press, 1991, 12. See also her more recent volume *In Search of Opera*, Princeton, Princeton University Press, 2001.

[18] Abbate is careful to introduce her foundational ideas, though, in a piece – for many, *the* piece – not of opera or music drama but of orchestral programme music, Paul Dukas's 'The Sorcerer's Apprentice'. See ibid., Chapter 2, 'What the Sorcerer Said', 30–60.

'Premonition' is particularly rich, it seems to me, in such different 'musics' of vocality, and the one I would like to discuss is the music of the 'person'. The voice begins, of course, with the word 'I', the orchestra in stasis, and the narrative and sound world of the voice immediately colonizing our attention. There is a second reference to the 'I' who is singing at the beginning of the second line of verse in bar 6, this time in harness with the fully engaged orchestra. The voice continues describing the world around her – the quietness of the doors, the streets, the heavy dust: here the voice loses person and gains narration, it might be said, and – as in film with the diagetic confluence of music understood as emanating directly from image viewed – we have what Abbate would call a different 'kind' or mode of music – the quietness reflected, for example, in the filigree instrumentation around bars 10 and 11, and above all in the motionless, heavy dust animated by the circling clarinet melody in bars 13–14 over quietly pulsating strings and a sustained bass sonority (see above, Ex. 3.3). Then, however, the voice returns to the person, not only telling us that she senses the storms, and is in herself moved by this, but in a moment of musicopoetic transubstantiation she suddenly describes the 'body', what is actually happening to her as a flag, although there is of course a double resonance or representation here – an embedded metonym, it can well be called – since the images of spreading, collapsing into oneself, hurling oneself, are after all powerful images of the *voice* that is expressing the female *body* that is expressing the flag.

Now, it needs to be stressed that it is what is *double* or *embedded* here that yields, or is yielded by, vocality. That there is an 'I' in the poem representing or represented by a 'flag' is just in the words. The words alone tell us of a simile, or something being 'like' something else, and this is precisely Rilke's poetic ploy when he begins the poem with 'I am like . . .' – a close textual analysis of the poem by itself as it begins! But only the poem as performed, say by a composer, can turn this something being 'like' something else into something *being* something else, into metonym; and I would say that only the female singer in her physical presence can seduce us into mapping one thing that is *like* another completely on to or into itself so that what we experience is a single, multidimensional entity.[19]

---

[19] I do not for a moment discount the reality of a reciter, including the reciter in one's own head, bringing about such poetic fusion. There is a tendency, which I need to acknowledge here without being able to do anything about it in this context, to assume in discussions of song vis-à-vis poetry that poetry is a quintessentially *written* form of art. One wonders, for example, despite Beate Perrey's recent elucidation of other important aspects of Robert Schumann's theory of song (see Beate Perrey, Chapter 5, 'Theories of Song: Schumann's "Higher Sphere of Art" ', of *Schumann's Dichterliebe and*

At this moment, incidentally, the singer sings the beautiful melodic curve G sharp, B, G from the orchestral opening, one of various points in this song that make Bryan Simms's epithet 'athematic' hard to take in.[20] And although the orchestra is sensitized to the text – for instance, in such a tiny detail as the quaver rest in bar 23 immediately following the word 'alone' – nevertheless, the diegetic moment has passed, the person of the voice has howled alone of her loneliness in the great storm, and the orchestra is charged with a truly Schumannian, wordless 'last word' that must, of course, bring this heady state of threat and impending chaos to an end.

It is at least open to debate whether the critic's role in response to Op. 22 is simplified or complicated by the existence of Schoenberg's own lecture, entitled 'Analysis of the Four Orchestral Songs Opus 22', written in German in 1932.[21] These coals have been raked over before, and they seem to me typically frustrating, typical of some of Schoenberg's thinking that came before the public in inchoate form. One writer, Kramer, does find a special point in this lecture:

> Commenting on his Four Orchestral Songs, Op. 22, Schoenberg himself once claimed that song is a rhythmic imitation of the movement between pitches that characterizes the voice in expressive speech. If he was right, then song is in essence a stylisation of the sound and feel of the self in its openness.[22]

Yet even taken at its most positive, Schoenberg's point is hardly clear (and Kramer's even less so). Does it really tell us anything more than is conveyed by the conventional term 'speech-rhythm', and is there, historically viewed, a genuine difference in kind between, say, the highly detailed speech-rhythm settings of a Schoenberg or perhaps even more successfully of a Janáček in the early twentieth century, however carefully crafted, and a composition of any good, typical eighteenth-century opera-recitative spinner?

Schoenberg's lecture is in any case full of apologies, or they are at least what might be called deferrals. When he says, for instance, that 'it is not

Early Romantic Poetics: Fragmentation of Desire, Cambridge, Cambridge University Press, 2002, 47–67), to what extent Schumann and other leading songsmiths of the nineteenth and twentieth centuries were thinking of poetry as a performed medium in the first place (see Brahms's advice to Jenner on songwriting, p. 43). Again we need to bear in mind Abbate's implied call (see p. 64) to watch out for the multifarious nature not only of our subjective interpretations, but also of the *object* of analysis itself.

20 Bryan Simms, *The Atonal Music of Arnold Schoenberg, 1908–1923*, Oxford, Oxford University Press, 2000, 150.

21 Arnold Schoenberg, 'Analysis of the Four Orchestral Songs Opus 22', in *Perspectives of New Music*, 3/2, Spring-Summer 1965, 1–21.

22 Lawrence Kramer, *Music and Poetry: The Nineteenth Century and After*, Berkeley, University of California Press, 1984, 131.

feasible . . . to present an analysis in the older sense by citing the main theme, subsidiary theme, development sections, repetitions, etc.' (3) because the poem in new music determines the form, I am not persuaded that he is making a good case that would distinguish his own Lied construction from, say, Schumann's. Or when he observes that in the second song of Op. 22 there is the same motive as in the first, 'but maybe that is no more than a coincidence?' (11), and then that the 'real connection is another one', but he does not care to speak about it because 'the result could hardly be in keeping with a piece such as this song', which he goes on to mention is extraordinarily short . . . well, there is a severe case of defensiveness here to which he has his right; and he may have even claimed that this was hard earned after his decades of critical battering, although in the end it appears to be merely some species of fruitless self-denial.[23] It is disappointing – and I am far from alone in feeling this, to judge from the literature – that this lecture, offering us the only such record of Schoenberg's relatively extensive contemplation of an atonal composition, is more political than polemical, and addressed to the unwilling audience, to Tovey's audience really (see note 16), rather than to the eager musician. This fits in with the pattern of Schoenberg's theorizing, which, viewed forensically, perhaps a little unsympathetically compared with the positive appraisals that were attempted in Chapter 1, does often have the feel of a significant body of lost opportunities.

Not so the music, which to this day, and even though as far as is known the composer never once heard it performed, Schoenberg experts regard as a masterpiece, however enigmatic.[24] I have tried to outline here the general sense in which this song stands as a shining example of Berg's idea about Schoenberg's music with its 'inexhaustible artistic techniques . . . the use of all compositional possibilities of the music of centuries: in short, its boundless opulence'.[25] Almost incidentally, in case the reader has been wondering what is Berg's answer to his own question that has been draped across this chapter, he answers it near the beginning by observing that if Schoenberg's music is 'so hard' to understand, this is the listener's fault:

Generally speaking, to understand this language in its entirety and details means recognizing the entrance, duration, and end of all melodies, hearing the

---

[23] I discuss some of the ideological subtexts in early Schoenberg criticism in '*Pierrot lunaire* and the Resistance to Theory', in *The Musical Times*, 1989, 130, 732–6, an essay that was designed to encapsulate in one case study the clearest kinds of historiographical contingency.
[24] See for example Dominique Jameux's admiring account of Op. 22 in his recent *L'Ecole de Vienne*, Paris, Fayard, 2002, 388–91.
[25] Berg, 'Why is Schoenberg's Music', 69.

simultaneous sounding . . . of the voices not as random occurrences, but as harmonies, and experiencing the small and large concatenations and contrasts as such. It means following a piece of music as a person with full command of the language follows the working of a piece of poetry. For one who is able to think musically, this is equivalent to understanding the work itself. Therefore, the question at the head of our investigation seems already answered if we can only succeed in examining Schoenberg's musical ways of expression for their intelligibility, and in determining the extent of their lucidity.[26]

Yet I also wanted to make the point once more from a distinctive perspective, and once more without being in a position to make it conclusively, that in a song, as opposed to the string quartet analyzed by Berg, such noumenal qualities must also and crucially lie – must in the end be found – in its vocality.

In this regard I would take a more variegated view than Julian Johnson in *Who Needs Classical Music?*, where he characterizes 'a work like . . . *Erwartung*' (close to Op. 22 chronologically and in its musical language) as still sounding 'prohibitively modern to many listeners'. 'Why does Schoenberg's music', he asks, and without doubt consciously echoing Berg's question about difficulty, 'exhibit so much fragmentation and complexity?' While his answer, that the 'lyrical, melodic aspect parts company with the harmonic system in which it was formally grounded',[27] is a perfectly sustainable generalization with which I have no difficulty in agreeing, it is also the case that the apparent fragmentation, a feature that has been called in a Boulezian spirit 'proliferation' here, coalesces around a shaft of sustained expressive clarity taking us from the first note to the last in a song like 'Premonition'. It was not for nothing that Schoenberg needed to be aware of his capacities at the time when he was questioning the very possibility of going on composing music that was truly 'modern' but also of truly Viennese structural integrity:

I continued to prefer composing music for texts, and I was still dependent purely upon my feeling for form. And I had to say to myself – and was perhaps entitled to do so – that my feeling for form, modelled on the great masters, and musical logic, which had been provided in so and so many cases, must guarantee that what I write is formally and logically correct, even if I do not realize it.[28]

It is in song in particular, and with music and text in general, that Schoenberg was able to tame what Johnson calls the composer's inherent 'complexity', because of the guaranteed focus of attention, the continuity of

---

[26] Ibid., 60.
[27] Julian Johnson, *Who Needs Classical Music?*, Oxford, Oxford University Press, 2002, 105.
[28] 'Analysis', 3.

narrative whether active or interrupted, and the textural consistency of the medium. The problem of defining an 'enhanced formalism', wrestled with extensively by, for instance, Lydia Goehr,[29] and of developing a critical language that truly does focus on the vocality of vocal music, meant nothing to a practitioner such as Schoenberg. Yet it is a vital project for music theory and analysis, especially in the face of masterpieces that we still rarely hear, and have barely assimilated into our image of early twentieth-century music.

[29] Lydia Goehr, *The Quest for Voice: On Music, Politics, and the Limits of Philosophy*, Oxford, Clarendon Press, 1998.

CHAPTER 4

Interlude on peace, laws, flowers, and men flying

Schoenberg appears again now as bridge into the future, to vocal music of the later twentieth century, in order to keep alive a narrative thread from the preceding chapters, and to do so there will be one break in the 'rule' of the narrative. Self-evidently this book is concentrating on the song of the solo voice. Song is also, though, at least in my hearing of how Western music ticks, an entity that presents in many forms. One has only to think of the aesthetics of piano playing from Mozart to Chopin and beyond, where making the *instrument* 'sing' is the highest perceived good, and this serves as a reminder of our starting point at the 'Song without Words' and a consideration of some of the twists and turns in what that idea did and could mean. Song can certainly be for vocal ensemble, of which Schoenberg's *Friede auf Erden* is an astonishing representative, choral music at the cutting edge of its compositional time, and raising issues of analytical interpretation not wholly dissimilar from those raised by song in its purest form, solo song. Yet although the 'solo' is plain enough in Cathy Berberian's *Stripsody*, which we shall be visiting as the end-stop of this chapter, it in turn raises the rather more gritty question of what is and what is not 'song' in the vocal sense. *Stripsody* is for soprano solo, yes: it is of about normal length:[1] it is continuous, and clearly plumbs some sort of 'heights' and 'depths' of human expression, even telling a story, at least in the spirit outlined in Chapter 1 (see pp. 19–21), bearing in mind that it is hardly possible for a narrative *not* to tell a story; and without doubt *Stripsody* requires virtuosic vocal technique in order to achieve an accomplished, convincing performance. It does not contain any real 'notes' such as one might normally recognize, however, so not surprisingly it is not in normal notation – any kind of normal notation. More of this to come.

---

[1] Berberian's recorded performance of *Stripsody* (issued in 1971, and remastered on CD as WER 60054–50) takes 4′ 33″, a period of time made universally famous through John Cage's 'silent' environmental piece *0′ 00″ 4′ 33″, solo for any player* of 1952, although as far as I am aware this is just one of those things.

In between we shall move through two moments in the history of vocal music that certainly were 'modern' a few decades ago, the one, Alexander Goehr's *The Law of the Quadrille* being recognizably in the Schoenbergian afterglow of later twentieth-century advanced rather than avant-garde composition, the other, György Kurtág's *The Sayings of Péter Bornemisza* also being a song cycle for voice and piano, but of Herculean length, and strangely of its own kind in any number of thought-provoking ways, starting with its curious designation as a 'Concerto for Soprano and Piano', and bearing enticing comparisons with Schumann. The Goehr and the Kurtág are roughly contemporaneous with Copland's revised (orchestrated) version of 'Going to Heaven!', which is the principal object of enquiry in Chapter 5, and which comes from a very distinct aesthetic landscape. If to some extent all this in Chapter 4 amounts to a hymn to diversity – the religious and sacred in Schoenberg and Kurtág as against, say, the decidedly secular in Goehr and Berberian, or the epitome of earnestness if exultation in Schoenberg and tragedy if transfiguration in Kurtág as against what may be called the playful in Goehr and the outright comic (as adjective, but also as a noun of both the object and the person) in Berberian – nevertheless, we shall not, knowingly, lose sight of the interplay of words and music, of the unifying question of what makes words sing in such diverse musics of these kinds.

PEACE

Schoenberg's *Friede auf Erden* (*Peace on Earth*) for mixed, *a cappella* voices was completed in 1907, at the zenith of the composer's first accomplishments in 'atonal' composition.[2] It was premiered four years later in Vienna. The circumstances of the composition of *Friede auf Erden* are of little specific interest. The circumstances of its premiere, offering a fascinating vignette of contemporaneous musicmaking,[3] do perhaps tell us a little about the content of this profound score. The music itself offers, on internal evidence, a remarkable insight into the transitional concerns of a work on the cusp of true atonality, and into Schoenberg's relationship to the text. Probably because there was such early debate about Schoenberg's perceived masterpieces, and because of his intense work in producing them and seeing them into actual performances, this relatively short composition took

---

[2] An earlier version of my comments on this music appeared in German in 'Friede auf Erden Op. 13', in *Arnold Schönberg: Interpretationen seiner Werke*, ed. Gerold Gruber, Laaber, Laaber-Verlag, 2002, 172–80.

[3] See F. C. Heller (ed.), *Arnold Schönberg, Franz Schreker Briefwechsel mit unveröff. Texten von Arnold Schönberg*, Schneider, Tützing, 1974, pp. 32–7.

some time to be heard and was discussed little in the literature of the second and third decades of the twentieth century, diverse, contentious and rather comprehensive though that Schoenberg literature would prove to be. What musicians of the time thought of *Friede auf Erden* was that it was a relatively minor work, and it was notoriously difficult to perform. There were rehearsals of it in 1908 under Franz Schalk, but the prospect of a premiere had to be abandoned. When the work was slated for its eventual premiere under Franz Schreker, the conductor asked Schoenberg for a string orchestra version to secure the choral intonation, and this is the origin of the composer's score for winds and strings completed in October 1911 and used in the premiere. In more modern times there have been many performances and recordings of the authentic, *a cappella* version, even if Op. 13 remains one of the most challenging scores of the modern choral repertoire.

In Anton von Webern, however, we get a clue to the important insights to be had into the fabric of this musical composition. 'Between the Chamber Symphony and Second String Quartet', he writes (and see p. 61 for a comment on that quartet), 'is [this] work of the most artistic polyphony, the most wonderful sonic effects, and the most sublime expression.'[4] There is no doubt that the polyphonic artistry here is of the highest order, and although the piece is rooted in conventional tonality (D minor/major, which along with E is Schoenberg's favoured tonal centre in those compositions where a feeling of tonality is evident; see also p. 63) its harmonic excursions are as rich as any of the radically chromatic progressions that Schoenberg constructs in order to illustrate the question discussed so penetratingly by Craig Ayrey of whether one can decide whether a passage is 'Tonal oder atonal?', that is, tonal or atonal, and Schoenberg's very idea of a schism or 'Scheideweg' between two worlds is precisely the wider, human topos of Conrad Meyer's poem 'Friede auf Erden'.[5]

---

[4] Anton von Webern, 'Schönbergs Musik', in [no author], *Arnold Schönberg mit Beiträgen von Alban Berg, Paris von Gütersloh, K. Horwitz, Heinrich Jalowetz, W. Kandinsky, Paul Königer, Karl Linke, Robert Neumann, Erwin Stein, Ant. v. Webern, Egon Wellesz*, publisher unknown, Munich 1912, 22–48; 36 (my translation). Webern had massive authority as one of the handful of truly major and influential composers of the twentieth century. From the large literature on his music it is worth mentioning an example of a detailed account of one of Webern's own songs, 'Sterne, ihr silbernen Bienen der Nacht', Op. 25, No. 3, in Christopher Wintle's 'Webern's Lyric Character', in *Webern Studies*, ed. Kathryn Bailey, Cambridge, Cambridge University Press, 1996, 229–63.

[5] For Ayrey's discussion of the analytical challenges inherent in transitional music of the Second Viennese school, including some analytical exegesis of Schoenberg's first 'Satire', Op. 28, and references to Schoenberg's theoretical discussions of the 'Tonal oder atonal?' issue, see his essay 'Berg's "Scheideweg": Analytical Issues in Op. 2/ii', in *Music Analysis*, 1/2, July 1982, 189–202; see in particular 193–5.

The poem dates from 1886 and will have been regarded by Schoenberg as a 'modern' allegory:

Peace on Earth
As they grazed their flock, the shepherds
bore the angel's salutation
through the lowly portal, onward
to the Mother and her Child.
Hosts of Heaven led the hymn,
through the starry spheres resounding,
Heaven led the song proclaiming,
'Peace, O Peace upon the Earth!'

Since that time of angels, warning
O how many deeds so bloody
has that armored horseman, Conflict,
on his wild horse brought forth!
On how many a holy night
sang the choir of spirits quaking,
pressingly yet softly pleading,
'Peace, O Peace upon the Earth!'

Yet survives belief eternal
that the weak shall not forever
fall as helpless victim to each
murd'rers[*sic*], fresh indignity.
Righteousness, or something kin,
weaves and works in rout and horror,
and a kingdom yet shall rise up
seeking Peace upon the Earth.

Slowly shall its form develop,
holy duties while fulfilling,
weapons free of danger forging,
flaming swords for cause of Right.
And a royal line shall bloom
mighty royal sons shall flourish,
whose bright trumpets peal proclaiming,
Peace, O Peace upon the Earth!
Translation © Bernard S. Greenberg 2001

We do not know precisely why Schoenberg turned his attention to this Christmas hymn of peace. Hermann Danuser argues convincingly that Op. 13 is an example of '*Weltanschauungsmusik*', a German neologism that expresses the idea of music expressing a personal philosophy, or perhaps one might call it 'positional music', alongside *Verklärte Nacht* in particular, but in a spirit that was common to many works of this period. Although Danuser is right to characterize *Friede auf Erden* as fin-de-siècle music in important respects, I argue below that it also offers glimpses of the modernist future through Schoenberg's twelve-note works and far beyond.[6] Hartmut Krones tries to persuade us that Op. 13 is at the end of a period in Schoenberg of heightened late Romanticism, a view with which I am in even less sympathy, although it is far from incomprehensible.[7]

What seems overriding is that the inherent duality of Op. 13, customarily described as a duality between the real world and an ideal world – for example between the 'many deeds so bloody' ('viele blut'ge Taten')[8] of verse 2 and the 'Peace' ('*Friede*') that appears in the poem no fewer than seven times, and each time in the final line of every verse – offered Schoenberg the prospect of just the kind of tension that had been so significant in, for instance, the programme poem by Dehmel of *Verklärte Nacht*.[9] We can ascribe to this tension the actual musical dualities that would be self-evident in anyone's analysis of this score. The minor/major duality is signalled by the key signatures of one flat in bars 1–10 and 32–88, and elsewhere two sharps.[10] Rhythmically, a sort of minim 'tactus', especially in the haunting 'Peace' refrains initiated at bar 22, is set against the rapid quaver movement in the imitative sections that we might call the 'bloody', 'murd'rers' [*sic*] and 'weapon' episodes at bars 38–46, 82–8 and 113–21 respectively. There is also a constructional duality between the driving, developmental style that is pervasive here and the ostinato stases, especially those using the 'Peace' motif that first appears in the bass starting in bar 11–12, after which the notes

[6] Hermann Danuser, 'Lyrik und Weltanschauungsmusik beim frühen Schönberg: Bemerkungen zu Opus 4 und Opus 13', in *Arnold Schönberg – Neuerer der Musik*, ed. Rudolf Stefan and Sigrid Wiesmann, Vienna, Lafite, 1996, 24–31.

[7] Hartmut Krones, 'Arnold Schönberg: Friede auf Erden, Op. 13', in *Österreichische Musikzeitschrift*, 53/3–4, 1998, 55–7.

[8] Where appropriate the German text will be given here as well as the English to enable some readers to identify these points of the score easily.

[9] It does not seem to have been noted in the literature on Schoenberg that the climactic reiterations of '*Friede*' in bars 149–50 (cf. also bars 70–2) are so close in musical gesture to the memorable cadential chords at the end of the first main section of *Verklärte Nacht* (including the notorious uncatalogued dissonance spotted by the *Tonkünstlerverein*, a committee that rejected the work for performance) as to be understood as a self-quotation, whether consciously or unconsciously, rather in the way that 'Valse de Chopin' from *Pierrot lunaire* is believed to 'quote' Op. 19, No. 4. See my *Schoenberg: Pierrot lunaire*, Cambridge, Cambridge University Press, 1992, 41.

[10] The score of this work is widely available in good music libraries. In the *Collected Works* it is A/V/18 (ed. T. Okuljar, 1980).

E–C sharp –F sharp –B appear no fewer than four further times in regular minims (this device recurs in bars 89–98, as it does in bars 137–48, where in addition the two final versions of the motif are augmented rhythmically to cover four bars of semibreves). We also find highly expressive extremes of register, so that, for example, the 'choir of spirits quaking' ('Chor der Geister zagend') of bars 53ff. is low and thickly textured with all voices at some stage singing in major and minor thirds, whereas in the final, ecstatic phase of this music the sopranos are taken up to high B (bars 142 and 152). One of many aspects of this work that render it extremely difficult to perform, apart from the simple difficulty of pitching it from one figure to the next and for the choir to maintain that pitch throughout, is the tessitura required of the voices. The Bass 2 part, for instance, ranges from E above middle C to D two octaves below; not so many choirs have basses capable of a genuine range of more than two octaves.

The duality is also represented in the contrast between homophony – basically, the voices singing in chords – and the polyphony that Webern found so 'artistic' (see above). The texture is largely polyphonic and imitative, not surprisingly for a work of this kind, and this, of course, is a rather different sort of essential vocality from those that we discuss elsewhere, one that the singers experience collectively by definition. At the very opening Schoenberg declares his hand with a texture involving three-part imitation (Tenor, Soprano in rhythmic diminution, then Bass in a quasifugal, 'dominant' tonal answer to Soprano) but the flowing lines and regular harmonic pace settle into a serene setting of 'Peace' to close the first verse (bars 21ff.), with Soprano and Alto in minims of celestial peace 'accompanied' by descending scalic passages in Tenor and Bass (which are, however, as one would expect in Schoenberg, shaped in such a way as to express the main motivic material of this piece). Similarly, the very end of the composition resolves into serene, albeit trenchant, block chords. Contrasted with this kind of simple, monumental beauty are passages that clearly delighted Webern in the sheer virtuosity of their polyphonic artifice. The final image of a world of heroes offers a case in point. At the line 'mighty royal sons shall flourish' ('Wird erblühn mit starken Söhnen'), the choir is not only split into eight parts (as frequently elsewhere in the piece, although naturally the writing rarely uses eight actual independent lines of music since there is often some degree of doubling), but these eight parts are linked in an astonishing imitative web in a passage that is purely diatonic, S1 having the 'scalic' material mentioned above, and T2 the 'Peace' minims ('canon' here is taken to mean imitation at pitch or at the octave):

Bar 126　　　　　　　127

S1

        S2 (canon of T2)

                A1 (inversion of S1)

                A2 (canon of B1)

        T1 (imitation of S1)

  T2   *B1 (inversion of T2)*

                B2 (imitation of S1)

Ex. 4.1:　Schoenberg, *Friede auf Erden,* canonic structure of bars 126–7

This chart shows that Schoenberg is constructing a 'double quadruple canon' in this extraordinary exercise of compositional virtuosity, one that aspires to a quite sculpted beauty through the interplay of maximal unity and diversity. What this demonstrates is a kind of integral collective vocality that is available only in a medium such as this. When Kurtág feels a corresponding polyphonic urge (if one may put it that way), he has no choice but to provide the inevitable textural proliferation in the piano, and it is this tendency perhaps above all others in Kurtág's approach that leads him into the danger – if such it is – of the piano dominating the expressive surface of the music, possibly, as we shall see, to 'an over-extending of its expressive powers' (see p. 106).[11] This feature of the Schoenberg is also a historical marker, for here we see the urge to variegated synthesis that would lead Schoenberg to such feats of construction in a chromatic rather than a diatonic context, to just the kind of chromatic proliferation that was noted in our study of 'Premonition' (Chapter 3). The passage is decidedly one of traditional counterpoint that Schoenberg would call 'Bachian'. He regarded the 'combination of superimposed themes' in later homophonic music as a different kind of counterpoint, where, for example, melodies use dissonant tones like consonances, and he points to the development

[11] Stephen Walsh, 'György Kurtág: An Outline Study (I)', in *Tempo,* 140, March 1982, 11–21; 16.

section of the First String Quartet and the Scherzo and Trio of the Second Quartet as examples of the latter.[12] Indeed the entire Second Viennese serial enterprise had its origins in this kind of elevation of canon to the level of single controlling principle.[13] To those who choose to be attuned to the wafting seeds of growth that come blown in a breeze that binds different historical points, this is a *locus classicus* of a future visible in the past. For Schoenberg and his pupils, freedom, the very essence of Meyer's text to which we shall be returning shortly, lies in the most ramified application of 'law' (which we shall see celebrated via Kafka in Goehr's *Quadrille* cycle), and in *Friede auf Erden* the balance of rule and fantasy is, I would submit, as compelling as can be found anywhere in Schoenberg's compositions.[14]

To a large extent the form of this work was always likely to be determined by the text, since Schoenberg has selected a poem that, although 'modern' as mentioned above, is highly stylized in its constructions, with four verses each consisting of eight lines more or less based on rhyming couplets, although with a subtle variation in the rhyme scheme that elevates this hymn beyond the dreary (but, let it be said, appropriate) predictability of ordinary festive poetry. This is obviously in a different realm from the 'love song' and the question of what a love song is like that was floated at the beginning of Chapter 2; and Danuser's term '*Weltanschauungsmusik*' (see p. 78) is certainly appropriate, not least with its political connotations.

The rhyme scheme is 1/abbccdda; 2/eeaffgga; 3/hhaiijja; 4/kkallmma. The actual words used as the 'a' rhyme motif are – cited in German here to show the continuity of word-sound – '*Herde*'[15] (flock, a reference that will arise again in a strikingly contrasting spirit in the Dickinson/Copland world of Chapter 5, but representing a pastoral trope that is ubiquitous in human art), '*Erde*' (earth), '*Pferde*' (horse), '*Erde*', '*Mordgebärde*' ('murd'rers . . . indignity' – that is, murderous conduct), '*Erde*', '*Fährde*' (danger), '*Erde*'. We can well imagine the delight with which Schoenberg contemplated

---

[12] Arnold Schoenberg, *Preliminary Exercises in Counterpoint*, London 1970 (2nd ed.), 224.

[13] It is especially in late Webern (Opp. 21–31) that this canonical principle has recently been not only identified but at last theorized in a thorough, convincing way. See especially Kathryn Bailey, *The Twelve-Note Music of Anton Webern*, Cambridge, Cambridge University Press, 1991; and Anne C. Shreffler, '"Mein Weg geht jetzt vorüber": The Vocal Origins of Webern's Twelve-Note Composition', in *Journal of the American Musicological Society*, 47, 1994, 275–339.

[14] Among those pupils were not only such as Webern who carried on the tradition of contrapuntal combination and derivation to previously unimagined levels, but also John Cage who turned from this tradition to the 'law' of the unconscious mind. The lively dialogue between Cage and Boulez is a remarkable testimony to this kinship; see Jean-Jacques Nattiez (ed.), *The Boulez–Cage Correspondence*, Cambridge, Cambridge University Press, 1993.

[15] Here I give the German words first for a self-evident reason.

this extremely euphonic and systematic verbal interplay, especially in a context where the highly singable word '*Friede*' (peace) appears many times. Christian Martin Schmidt argues that Schoenberg is concerned above all with the formal idea of Meyer's text rather than with a literal rendition.[16] This is an understandable interpretation, even if we have been discussing extensively from the start of this book questions that will lead anyone to ask what can ever be thought to be literal about the way words are set in any context. In any case, it seems to me that the one factor, the 'idea' of a text, does not need to be weighed against the other, which broadly speaking may be thought of as the way the words shape the musical surface, and, of course, vice versa. Here – as in Schoenberg's Lieder in general, as in, for instance, *Pierrot lunaire* or *Erwartung* that are both for solo voice and ensemble, and, of course, in his incomplete magnum opus, the opera *Moses und Aron* – there is no need to suppose that his dogged pursuit through a literary text of its 'idea', the '*Gedanke*' in German, somehow deflects his compositional attention from the finest surface details of the word-setting and instrumental support and commentary, both technically and, so to speak, semantically.

In addition to the 'verbal interplay' just discussed, Meyer's poem offers rich imagery. In verse 1 the Christmas scene is set and the choir singing the last line 'Peace, O Peace upon the Earth!' is, we have just been told, none other than the 'Hosts of Heaven' (a pleasant thought for the actual singers themselves; see comments on bars 21ff. above). In verse 2 the vicissitudes of the real world, of, for instance, 'that armoured horseman, Conflict' (line 3), offer Schoenberg the opportunity for animated, highly chromatic music that has about it the bustling intensity of Bach's Passion crowd scenes (e.g., the 'Crucify' chorus from the St Matthew Passion). In Schoenberg's brave new world, however, the poetic vicissitudes also offer the opportunity for chromatic saturation, as the following account of the pitch content of bars 38^2-41^1 illustrates (for convenience $0 = C$, $1 = C$ sharp, etc.; Altos, Tenors and Basses are divisi when double figures appear). In the lowest line in Ex. 4.2, there is an attempt at a rough harmonic analysis, although admittedly any listener is likely to perceive something different in this fleeting passage, depending on the extent to which context, the kind of 'distance hearing' we were discussing in Chapter 2, is taken into account. However that may be, note that in the space of merely $1\frac{1}{2}$ bars the chromatic aggregate of all twelve available pitches is completed at '*'.

---

[16] Christian Martin Schmidt, 'Zukunftsverheissung und musikalische Zielgerichtetheit: Arnold Schönbergs Chor Friede auf Erden op. 13', in *Berliner Beiträge zur Mussikwissenschaft: Beihefte zur Neuen Berlinischen Musikzeitung*, 9/1, 1994, 40–5.

S									5	6	1	0	10
A	11 0 5 4 1 3 3 2*							11 0	8 7				
	7 8 1 0 9 11 11 10*							7 8	5 4				
T	8 8 6					4 5 0 1			4 5 11			
						0 1 10 8				0 1 8			
B	4 5 1 0 6 8 8 7								7	8	4		
									4	5	0			

[f: I-   ?II-   I-   V-   I   (-IV
                                                                at 41$^{3-4}$)]

Ex. 4.2: Schoenberg, *Friede auf Erden,* pitch structure of bars 38–41

Verse 3 moves on to a more abstract plane, and here Schoenberg is at his most commanding in ensuring that the musical structure complements the narrative in that unique way music has of being able to offer a *polyphony* of articulation, which is not a matter we are considering in general elsewhere in these pages. The first four lines beginning 'Yet survives belief eternal' are swept along in a four-part fugal texture that transforms into three parts accompanying Sopranos in a kind of quaver arabesque with mostly four different lines of text sounding at any point – it is an exciting, expectant passage that is to lead to a masterstroke. At the words 'Righteousness, or something kin' – 'righteousness' for the German *'Gerechtigkeit'*, being for Schoenberg such a grounding concept in the ideal of freedom based on law[17] – Altos begin what turns out to be, as will be discussed later, the reprise of the quasi-sonata form of Op. 13. The Bass ostinato here (bars 89ff.; see above) underpins the upper parts with the 'Peace' motive in minims, and thus necessarily (although it is impossible to say whether Schoenberg's musical conception here was triggered by the musical or the textual device) they begin this passage with the second couplet of the final quatrain of the

[17] 'Justice' is the most literal translation.

verse. With astonishing control of his compositional materials, Schoenberg has contrived the inspired co-occurrence of the words 'Righteousness, or something kin' ('Etwas wie Gerechtigkeit') together with 'and a kingdom yet shall rise up' ('Und ein Reich will sich erbauen'). The ideal and the real, or potentially real, world counterpoint and support each other in a majestic synthesis of word with word and music with music.

Finally, in verse 4, which obviously Schoenberg is going to build to a glorious climax, there is the opportunity (bars 113ff.) for a multiple celebration of 'weapons free of danger forging' ('Waffen schmieden ohne Fährde'), with the upper voices expressing the ideal aspect in exultant legato, and the lower voices initiating a five-beat, quaver-based figure that almost shouts as it passes through each pair of voices (bars 113–16), followed by the double quadruple canon and subsequent Bass ostinato both analysed above.

There is certainly some sense in which the verse structure provides a four-section framework overall: bars 1–31; 31–75; 75–99; 100–60. From this (and bearing in mind that although there are tempo fluctuations in each verse the basic speed of the work is maintained) we can see that Schoenberg has taken a fairly routine approach to the proportions, delivering the text at a steady rate but putting the proportional weight on the final, epiphanic verse. There are, however, clear subsections as follows: 1–31 / 31–46; 46–75 / 75–88; 89–99 / 100–12; 113–21; 122–31; 131–44; 145–60. However different analysts may interpret the detailed articulation of the musical surface, it is also apparent that there is a sonata principle at work in terms of formal continuity. Clearly there is a reprise of the opening material (and mood) from bar 89, which as noted above occurs in the middle of a verse (with the second quatrain of verse 3), so that Schoenberg is using the text to provide an enjambment across a division of the musical form. This reading positively invites us to see the quaver figures beginning at bar 38 as contrasting, 'second theme' material, and thus possibly to see the whole section from bar 32, which is the beginning of verse 2, as the second element of a sonata exposition. The return of imitative quaver figures at bar 113 – the 'weapons' ('*Waffen*') section pointed to above – signals, then, the reprise of the second element, and following the diatonic 'imitative web' (see Ex. 4.1 and its associated comments), which provides a resounding closure of the tonal structure in D, bars 131 to the end can be regarded as a formal coda; structure and confirmatory poetry come together, as the sonata tradition is reconfirmed in musical terms, and as the real world of 'mighty royal sons . . . whose . . . trumpets peal' ('Söhnen, dessen helle Tuben dröhnen') comes together with the ideal world of 'Peace, O Peace upon the Earth!' ('Friede, Friede auf der Erde!').

But in what sense analytically is Op. 13 an example of sonata form? If by sonata form we mean the historical practice codified with such unique insight by Schenker as a binary form with an interrupted 'Fundamental Line' that at the reprise returns to the 'Primary Melodic Note' in order then to fulfil its inevitable 'structural descent' to the final tonic, the interruption supported by a Dominant 'Divider' in the bass, or at least the second most prominent Dominant of the bass arpeggiation,[18] then no, *Friede auf Erden* does not conform, which is hardly surprising of Schoenberg at one of his most fertile and groundbreaking periods of progressive composition. If, however, we mean by sonata form a structure with a 'tonic' varied reprise, and the varied reprise of secondary contrasting material, with a 'development' preceding the reprise, and (as was Brahms's practice) a decisive closing section (a developmental 'coda'), then we see another breeze blowing to the future here, for such a description would be equally apt for the *Piano Piece* (*Klavierstück*), Op. 33a, which Schoenberg was to complete at the height of his dodecaphonic powers some twenty-seven years later.

In summary, what makes this music sing is something perhaps even more elusive than has been encountered in earlier pages, at least in that this is a case where there is simply no choice but to analyse the music as a textural totality – there is no 'melody' here that can be isolated for study from its 'accompaniment', with the kind of transvocal theoretical urge that we often find applied to song and to vocal music in general. The expression of the words is integrally a function of where and how they occur in the music, as we saw with the choice example of the climactic point where Schoenberg delivers two parts of the text simultaneously, but also, I would say, perfectly lucidly and comfortably in the tradition of operatic vocal ensemble (or its equivalent in oratorio and other sacred genres), madrigal and part-song. With its barely perceivable diatonic backdrop, this music also needs, so Schoenberg evidently felt, formal clarity – a sort of monumental blocking-out and correlation of the overall elements that suits its ecstatic, incantatory, and as Schmidt would have it 'philosophical' or at least 'positional' inclination, music that makes a statement through its text and through its adoption of the mien of that text, its bearing, its manner. It does not draw us in filmically to a personal story as does 'Von ewiger Liebe' (see Chapter 2), it does not ask probing questions at the last moment, as with Schubert's cameo of love and Copland's journey to heaven to be experienced in Chapter 5, it does not boil down the text to an

---

[18] See Chapter 2, pp. 44–50, for a concrete illustration in Brahms of this Schenkerian picture of organic contrapuntal-structural tonal prolongation.

intaglio like 'Premonition' (*Friede auf Erden*, although not a long piece, is inherently 'developmental' in many ways as described or implied above), and it neither plays nor howls nor makes us laugh (I am referring here to the Goehr, Kurtág and Berberian in the pages immediately below). It is ensemble music of deep dignity from which we can learn something of the essence of the vocal through what only people coming together can do.

LAWS

'People' – or, let us say, 'how it is', to use Beckett's pithy title of a novella – are the concern, too, of Goehr's *The Law of the Quadrille*.[19] Franz Kafka fragments (from his *Wedding Preparations in the Country*) were set by Goehr (b. 1932) in the 1979 song cycle *Das Gesetz der Quadrille* (*The Law of the Quadrille*), for low voice and piano Op. 41. The texts are highly symbolic, as so often with the Czech writer of such well-known stories as *Metamorphosis* (where the narrator, an insurance salesman, awakes to discover that he has become a hideous beetle left to die): they are symbolic in being relatively bare of narrative colour, of intricacies within the 'plot', and bare of 'asides', or of much complicity with the reader at all by way of what Roland Barthes described as the 'prattle of meaning'.[20] The texts Goehr uses, severally or taken as a whole, are also correspondingly open to interpretation. I doubt that the many audiences who have been and will be moved by this song cycle can come away with an untroubled, crystalline sense of what Kafka wanted us to understand by 'the quadrille' and of what Goehr has made of his own understanding. Very clearly, though, there is a stern aura hovering around the rich visual and sonic images. It would surely be difficult to absorb this work textually through the music with open ears and an open mind while avoiding the feeling that one is not only being offered and shown something, but also 'told' something; something not necessarily philosophical, but a little rabbinically, it may be. Danuser's idea of '*Weltanschauungsmusik*' (see pp. 78–9) comes to mind once again, although compared with *Friede auf Erden* the *Quadrille* texts are decidedly secular in general, having more in common with the tradition of Hauff and Grimm Romantic fairy tales.

'The Law of the Quadrille'. So, what is this 'law'? One route towards some understanding of an answer might be to ponder – or for some readers

---

[19] An earlier version of my comments on Goehr's Kafka cycle appeared in 'All the Dancers know it and it is Valid for All Times: Goehr, Kafka and *The Law of the Quadrille*', in *Sing, Ariel: Essays and Thoughts for Alexander Goehr's Seventieth Birthday*, ed. Alison Latham, Aldershot, Ashgate, 2003, 171–9.
[20] Roland Barthes, *S/Z*, New York, Hill and Wang, 1974 [1970], 78–9.

who know this unforgettable little story to ponder again – Kafka's justifiably renowned text, the parable 'Before the Law', which presents a puzzling, rich, saddening, timeless, although also undoubtedly highly personal scenario. Unlike the fragments assembled by Goehr for *The Law of the Quadrille*, the nevertheless closely related 'Before the Law' tells a complete 'story', at least in that it offers a continuous narrative; although, not surprisingly of Kafka, and not surprisingly of his war-ravaged era of anxiety, we are driven by the seemingly painfully drawn skeleton of what *is* said to try to reconstruct and ponder the whole potential network of what is not:

Before the Law stands a doorkeeper. To this doorkeeper there comes a man from the country and prays for admittance to the Law. But the doorkeeper says that he cannot grant admittance at the moment. The man thinks it over and then asks if he will be allowed in later. 'It is possible,' says the doorkeeper, 'but not at the moment.' Since the gate stands open, as usual, and the doorkeeper steps to one side, the man stoops to peer through the gateway into the interior. Observing that, the doorkeeper laughs and says: 'If you are so drawn to it, just try to go in despite my veto. But take note: I am powerful, and I am only the least of the doorkeepers. From hall to hall there is one doorkeeper after another, each more powerful than the last. The third doorkeeper is already so terrible that even I cannot bear to look at him.' These are difficulties the man from the country has not expected; the Law, he thinks, should surely be accessible at all times and to everyone, but as he now takes a closer look at the doorkeeper in his fur coat, with his big sharp nose and long, thin, black Tartar beard, he decides that it is better to wait until he gets permission to enter. The doorkeeper gives him a stool and lets him sit down at one side of the door. There he sits for days and years. He makes many attempts to be admitted, and wearies the doorkeeper by his importunity. The doorkeeper frequently has little interviews with him, asking him questions about his hopes and many other things, but the questions are put indifferently, as great lords put them, and always finish with the statement that he cannot be let in yet. The man, who has furnished himself with many things for his journey, sacrifices all he has, however valuable, to bribe the doorkeeper. The doorkeeper accepts everything, but always with the remark: 'I am only taking it to keep you from thinking you have omitted anything.' During these many years the man fixes his attention almost continuously on the doorkeeper. He forgets the other doorkeepers, and this first one seems to him the sole obstacle preventing access to the Law. He curses his bad luck, in his early years boldly and loudly; later, as he grows old, he only grumbles to himself. He becomes childish, and since in his yearlong contemplation of the doorkeeper he has come to know even the fleas in his fur collar, he begs the fleas as well to help him and to change the doorkeeper's mind. At length his eyesight begins to fail, and he does not know whether the world is really darker or whether his eyes are only deceiving him. Yet in his darkness he is now aware of the radiance that streams inextinguishably from the gateway of the Law. Now he has not very long to live. Before he dies, all his experiences in these long years gather themselves in his head to one point, a question he has not yet asked the doorkeeper. He waves him nearer, since he can no longer raise his stiffening body. The doorkeeper has to bend low toward him, for the difference in height between them has altered much to the man's disadvantage. 'What do you want to know now?' asks the doorkeeper; 'you are insatiable.' 'Everyone strives to reach the Law,' says the man, 'so how does it happen that for all these many years no one but myself has ever begged for admittance?' The doorkeeper recognizes that the man has reached his end, and, to let his failing senses catch the words, roars in his ear: 'No one else could ever be admitted here, since this gate was made only for you. I am now going to shut it.'[21]

This parable was printed in 1916, about two years after Kafka wrote the novel *The Trial* in which it appeared (the novel itself was not published until 1925). 'Before the Law' came out again in German in Kafka's selected essays and aphorisms in 1934. On and on it lived in the proliferation of Kafka in the last century, long after the author had first mentioned it in his *Diaries*, on 13 December 1914, writing of his 'contentment and a feeling of happiness as the "Legend" ["Before the Law"] in particular inspires in me'.[22]

Contentment? Meaning that Kafka has, pleasurably, found expression for and resignation in just not knowing? Not knowing how to go inside a special place? How to be free? How to escape death, or even to make death seem worth while? Or is this rather a parable of obsession, immobilization, anticreativity: a modern moral tale of the peril of personal stasis? The latter reading is entirely plausible, to the extent that we think we are ever able to see inside the creative mind – or see into anyone's mind for any purpose. Seeing into Goehr's mind, if one can, one finds his same kind of detached contentment on having found expression even when it may be the expression of knowing only about what he might call the rhythm of doing things. Here, in the following quotation from Goehr, we are moving from textual moment and narrative character to the composer's idea of a 'piece' or pieces of music, and Goehr is talking, one may presume, as much about his feeling for his transvocal (pure) music as for the particular song cycle that one nevertheless suspects he has in mind in view of the specific Kafka reference:

Kafka writes in his *Notebooks*: 'The law of the Quadrille is clear, all the dancers know it and it is valid for all times. But one or other of the hazards of life, which ought not to, but over and over does, occur, brings you alone out of step. But you do not know, you know only your own bad luck.' Here, he finely expresses what I have . . . merely called a rise and fall in tension, the feeling of equanimity and harmoniousness when an action is carried out correctly and of 'bad luck' when it goes wrong.[23]

---

[21] *The Collected Short Stories of Franz Kafka*, Harmondsworth, 1988, 3–4.   [22] Ibid., 467.
[23] Alexander Goehr, *Finding the Key: Selected Writings of Alexander Goehr*, ed. Derrick Puffett, London, Faber, 1998, 221.

At least in moving between the poles of equanimity and bad luck Goehr is dancing, musically, rather than sitting frozen for life in front of narrative secrets that, it turns out (in 'Before the Law'), were always there for the taking – perhaps. His measured, sanguine words here are appropriately shorn of the ecstatic discourse one sometimes receives from composers revelling in their recall of the white heat of musical creation.

Goehr's cool compositional approach, at one level, in *The Law of the Quadrille* reflected this later, affirmatory musing. He was far from transfixed by Kafka, and it is important to understand that his approach was artistic, craft-driven as well as inspired, not representing any kind of phlegmatic pragmatism; in spite of his fascination with the East, so strongly signalled in his compositions (both textually and in musical ideas and procedures) as well as in his writings and teachings, we should not slip, either, into thinking of Goehr's as some kind of culturally adopted air of fatality. His attitude is more one of inner balance (as articulated, from the other side of the couch, by the psychoanalyst and writer Adam Phillips, who in *On Kissing, Tickling and Being Bored* tells of saying to a young patient objecting to further mention of a muddling matter that he may need to mention it, but if so he would warn her so that she could put her fingers in her ears):[24] being able to put your fingers in your ears is an important talent, a present-day version of Karl Kraus's (Goehr's so-admired Kraus's) 'I don't like to meddle in my private affairs.'[25] Again, contentment, detachment, equanimity are in the air. We are somewhere in the middleground between the elation of living life, including all possible future life, to the full as in 'Going to Heaven' (see Chapter 5), or, as we shall encounter in the next section, joining Bornemisza in a 'celebration' of the terrors of human existence.

What could follow, then, is an account of the radiances Goehr somehow reflects outwards from his Op. 41, the Law he espies and, as it were, exhales. This composition invites discussion of the interplay of tonality and atonality, of the 'song cycle' legacy and the particular aspects of that which may arise when setting a text in its original German, of structure (as when the eighth of the nine songs gives us a developed reprise of the first song, which already drew attention to the tonality/atonality struggle within the Law), and of voices from the past that are wafted onwards (not only the obvious ones, but, for example, in the four-bar passage from sixteen bars before the end with a clear – to me – echo of the piano postlude from Schumann's *Dichterliebe*, although here actually sung; see my comments on Kurtág and

---

[24] Adam Phillips, *On Kissing, Tickling and Being Bored*, London, Faber, 1993, 14.
[25] Karl Kraus, *Half-Truths and One-and-a-Half Truths*, ed. H. Zohn, Manchester, Carcanet, 1986, 42.

the opening of *Dichterliebe*, pp. 99–100). But rather than discussing influence and history even further, the focus here will be on the immanent in the attempt to catch something of the vocality of a work that is in many respects exceptionally transparent, and in this akin to what we shall be finding in Copland.

Among the various striking features of Song 1 is that the voice does have something of the demeanour of the gatekeeper, uttering only little things (three short, diatonic phrases), in a kind of celebratory declaration: it sings that the law is clear, all participants know it, and it holds for all time; one could hardly imagine a greater contrast to the explosive entrance of Tarzan at the beginning of *Stripsody* (see Ex. 4.9). Switching from accompanist to protagonist, the piano begins its elaboration with what the composer himself would have been likely to call an 'opposite', the urgent transformation shown in Ex. 4.3 of x into x1, underneath its new ascending thought, y. The

Ex. 4.3: Goehr, *Das Gesetz der Quadrille,* opening

piano finds no decisive response, but broods its *morendo* way to repetitive half-cadencing, somewhat in the same way that (some may think) the first and second songs of *Dichterliebe* are joined.

Song 1 will return as the beginning of Song 8, hugely reinterpreted in our minds after the welter of intervening musicopoetic images, strengthened following our experiences in Songs 2–7 of how people step out of line and how weird things happen all around us. And when the full law of the quadrille is revealed here, it turns out that it was merely as stated. The singer tells us, in what one may as well call an 'expressionist' *parlando*, that things happen, you find yourself out of place, and all you know is that it was bad luck. The piano, not entirely accompanying but adding its own obsessional assent (madness after all being inevitably tinged with the boring because of the underlying repetitiveness of its nonthinking process), nevertheless achieves that taxing, technical compositional task of sustained and entrancingly perceptible syncopation (score, pp. 32–3), and, of course, again one cannot but think of Schumann.

Goehr thus decided to enclose or, as it is called in literature, frame Kafka's (and his own) wild images, I suspect so that we can indulge in them unreservedly in the untamed, interior landscape of *Das Gesetz der Quadrille* (Songs 2–7), if in a thoughtful, learning way that adds to the raw experience itself. This sense of containment just on the edge represents Charles Baudelaire's idea of the modern (the poet more or less invented the term in his aesthetic writings of about 1860) translated into the late twentieth century: 'modern' is not what is recent, Baudelaire insisted in his radical new insight, but what is new, 'the ephemeral, the fugitive, the contingent, the half of art whose other half is the eternal and the immutable'.[26] And though one may think that Goehr made it easy for himself in choosing Kafka, and though he inevitably is somehow able to endow his own art with Kafka's modernist genius, the result, embodying such a risk in setting words that themselves ask so many questions, could have been a complete flop in lesser compositional hands. Vocality here is taken to a different level than that of the philosophical or the positional in their Romantic and post-Romantic senses (of which Danuser is thinking; see pp. 78–9). You might even feel that because the text is so inherently questioning and therefore inherently verbal (for there is no 'interrogative' in music?) it always threatens to float free from the fusion of music and text that might ideally be thought to form some kind of 'third' language (see Introduction, in particular p. 5). 'One of Kafka's intentions', writes the critic Franz Kuna, is 'to portray generally

---

[26] Charles Baudelaire, *The Painter of Modern Life and Other Essays*, London, Phaidon, 1964, 12.

dialectical relationships rather than allow his characters to arrive at one-sided views of reality, however "workable". In this way even the function of art itself becomes dual . . . The invitation is not to judge whether one extreme is better than the other; still less to affect a compromise by taking an abstract view of things',[27] sentiments with which everything we know about Goehr suggests he would agree enthusiastically. In internalizing the text of something like the *Quadrille* cycle as part of the musical experience, the listener is left *pensive*, and this is after all not a purely musical state but one that encapsulates what a complete human experience such as vocality can bring about in a way that is closed to monodimensional art.

In this existential context, if I may call it that, we are offered superb images set in something akin to the 'light, satirical' tone that Schoenberg had in mind for *Pierrot lunaire*, even if, like Schoenberg, Goehr has a recurrently unsmiling countenance here, drawn from his personal experience of what it is like to be a musician always slightly out of line – although why that perceived 'line', that idealized cultural dance, has mattered so much to Goehr is a different and more biographical story, a context for the *Quadrille* that it simply carries within itself (as for Kafka, too) without in any way parochializing the work. These images may best be measured against their extreme forms. At the subdued end Song 7 yields up the most apparently reserved 'affect' – a brief song about, as the text has it, 'what really matters', appropriately quiescent musically after the expansive preceding scenarios and before the reprise/revelation of Song 8.

Yet we must measure them, too, in their most vivid representations, say in the veiled, closing 'chorale' (this is my hunch about the generic compositional reference here) summoning a great detachment of not even loss itself, but only the memory of loss, summoning the soul's winter:

> The year of mourning was over,
> the birds' wings were limp.
> The moon bared herself in cool nights.
> Almond and olive had long been ripe.

A Mediterranean reverie, then, partaking in the twentieth century's ubiquitous spirit of lament?[28] Something perhaps Italianate that Kafka shares as an index of nostalgia (or better, sheer pastness) with many of his forebears, and above all Goethe, and that maybe Goehr draws on, too, in brushing,

---

[27] Franz Kuna, 'The Janus-faced Novel: Conrad, Musil, Kafka, Mann', in *Modernism 1890–1930*, ed. Malcolm Bradbury and James McFarlane, Harmondsworth, Penguin Books, 1991, 443–52; 450.
[28] 'Lament' is discussed recurrently in Arnold Whittall, *Exploring Twentieth-Century Music: Tradition and Innovation*, Cambridge, Cambridge University Press, 2003.

for instance, against Desdemona's very '*Salce*' ('willow') notes D and B from Verdi's *Otello* here at the word '*Nächten*' ('nights' – cool ones). Or, perhaps, at the burlesque end of the range of the vivid we can hear the cycle beginning its wild inner stories in Song 2 with romping hunting dogs (following Goehr's three raps in the piano's bass; threes are one 'law' of this composition, reminding us of an oriental drum and also the stick that strikes a French stage to initiate dramatic action), and then the almost relentless whirling semiquavers that, we will learn at the end of Song 2, were all part of the 'weightless merry journey', cutting filmically between soft and loud before the final, exhausted fade-out.

If that presages heights of expression, and the '-ism' and '-istic' tropes of 'expression-' into which critical habit will always tend to seduce us, they will emerge most overtly in Song 6, the raven song, a tirade, no lament, with both voice and piano struggling to contain the manic reaction that inescapable image-repetition ('why are you always in my path?') will generate, although even here (see Ex. 4.4) there is something consolatory in Goehr's warm harmonies that takes them decades forward from Schoenberg's 1912 brutalities (thinking, not surprisingly, of Pierrot's *Kreuze*).

And this tirade has been a foil for the still centre of the cycle, Song 5, where Kafka most directly addresses his reader, as does Goehr his listener, with an intense and epic lyricism rekindling an essential strand of the Lied tradition; Goehr has written that 'progress depends on self-knowledge and self-knowledge is best, possibly only, to be obtained by confronting oneself with the difficult tasks which our forefathers devised for us'.[29] So intense indeed is the lyrical elaboration here that Goehr needs to contain it by rather extensive varied repetition (compare, for example, the piano bars 5ff., 15ff. at t4, and bars 29ff. at t8, so that this musical material has partitioned the octave symmetrically at three pitch levels).

Before that were two remarkable 'inventions', in J. S. Bach's sense of the dogged and (in a musical rather than logical meaning) exclusive drawing out of musical narrative from short musical objects (which may be one kind of action that Schoenberg implied by his concept of the musical 'idea' or thought, the '*Gedanke*'; see p. 83). In the best post-Baroque music, and as Schubert above all bequeathed to subsequent worthwhile law-breakers, such musical objects can stand seemingly almost any amount of repetition. As Theodor Adorno put it so succinctly in his essay to celebrate the centenary of Schubert's death, 'the repeatability of Schubertian details stems from

---

[29] Alexander Goehr, 'What's Left to be Done?', in *The Musical Times*, 140/1867, Summer 1999, 19–28; 23.

Ex. 4.4: Goehr, *Das Gesetz der Quadrille,* Song 6, extract

their timelessness'.[30] Thus in Song 4, the 'Negro' driven mad by alienation and playing pranks on Europeans who mistakenly take this to be genuine African dance – so the alienated, as it were, alienates back – generates music based on the apposition of stomping, ritualistic beats with three-note infills and whizzing, proportionally asymmetrical roulades (flights, mental 'fugue').

---

[30] Theodor Adorno, 'Schubert', in *Gesammelte Schriften*, vol. xvii, Frankfurt, Suhrkamp, 1997, 18–33; 32 (my translation).

Ex. 4.5: Goehr, *Das Gesetz der Quadrille,* Song 4, opening

Previously, in Song 3, the astonishing text of which is sufficiently concise
to be quoted here in full, Goehr's apposition is at a formal level:

> In amazement we beheld the great horse.
> It broke the roof of our room.
> The cloudy sky was drifting faintly along its mighty outline,
> and its mane flew, rustling, in the wind.

One clomping idea (loud chords and their wistful echoes) tells us of the
'great horse', I suppose, and their celestial transformation controls the

middle section from the upbeat to bar 15, the two coming together in artful symbiosis for the end of the third and last line.

Let us briefly review the extracts shown here from the point of view of vocality. In Ex. 4.3, which shows the opening of Goehr's *The Law of the Quadrille*, the voice is clearly making some kind of historical reference to tonal music and is summoning a lost world, although it is a world we cannot easily identify – who would be surprised if a singer decided to put a little trill by way of seventeenth- or eighteenth-century-style ornamentation on the F on the downbeat of the second full bar? Immediately the 'voice of the piano' takes over in a post-tonal idiom that is elaborate and straining in the way we are familiar with from music that is rightly called 'expressionist' (see also p. 92), and so Goehr is setting up a dialogue with the potential for extensive stylistic development. One of the evocative qualities of this opening is the way in which the vocality of the first statement is at once seen to be a 'frame' from another age that comes to be reflected at a larger level in the framing contemporaneous roles of Songs 1 and 8 (see p. 94). And as we shall see in Chapter 5 in looking at both Schubert and Copland, the 'voice of the piano' has a strong pedigree in Western song – Lawrence Kramer goes so far, in discussing Schumann song, as to coin the choice aphorism (which although an exaggeration, inevitably, is nevertheless on target in important respects and rehearses here the opening thoughts of Chapter 1 above) 'a "song without words" but with words'.[31]

In Ex. 4.4, from Song 6, the raven song, what was called 'struggling' leads the voice to break out from sung notes to one explosive moment of *Sprechstimme*, on the word '*Lästig*' (which means annoying or troublesome), amid a welter of piano invention expressing, I would say, a kind of personalized frustration (called 'manic' above) rather close to the manner that is frequent, almost a hallmark, in the Kurtág to be discussed shortly. Ex. 4.5 is mostly instrumental but the listener can easily perceive in context the way that it passes through the essence of Goehr's 'oppositional' kind of invention where vocality – text-setting or 'representation' here, at least – is a function of the engagement between ideas of sharp individual identity, the grit in the oyster, the man and the doorkeeper in Kafka's story 'Before the Law', where note that everything hangs not only and obviously on what happens (come to the door, sit by the door, die) but crucially on what is *said*: without its last line – 'this gate was made only for you. I am now going

---

[31] Lawrence Kramer, *Music and Poetry: The Nineteenth Century and After*, Berkeley, University of California Press, 1984, 131.

to shut it' – that story would be something and nothing; how might it be sung?

FLOWERS

It is surely not too much in the vein of coffee-table history to imagine that if anyone could set Kafka's last line for voice, and find it a natural thing to attempt, it would be György Kurtág. Kurtág (b. 1926) has embraced some of the most refractory of modern texts including not only Kafka ('Kafka Fragments', Op. 24, 1987) but also Beckett whose poetry we encountered in Chapter 1 (for example 'What is the Word?', Op. 30b, 1991), Hölderin and Celan. This is a composer who is drawn to the intensity of fragmented allusion in language, and for whom challenges to verbal understanding seem to be the very air he breathes. Of the 'Kafka Fragments' Arnold Whittall writes:

> Consisting of thirty-nine, mainly tiny, movements divided into three parts, this is by no means the most demanding of Kurtág's cycles to perform, but it encapsulates the spell-binding dramatic and lyric character of his work. These are intimately personal texts, and the music, varying in notation from strict to (relatively) free, responds with an uninhibited directness to the verbal imagery, in a way that is both explicitly illustrative and also alert to the psychological drama that the words reflect.[32]

Kurtág's is a kind of vocality, in other words, that aims to capture both the surface and the 'message' of the words, and it does so not through artifice, device or a kind of compositional liturgy that we recognize and to which we respond as celebrants of the same cultural paradigms (which is a somewhat verbose way of characterizing the *Friede auf Erden* experience); but on the contrary it shocks, which is another way of putting what Whittall soberly identifies as Kurtág's 'uninhibited directness'. It is plain to all who experience performances of Kurtág's vocal music that in their ritual, mystical, ecstatic manner, which the composer himself has typically extended to the ways in which the music is to be interpreted and 'staged', there is a striving for a level of vocality as uncommon as it is demanding of the listener, a Modernism foregrounding, as Baudelaire put it, not what is recent, but what is new (see p. 92).

If anyone were asked to discuss 'the voice of the piano' in the Lied, it is hard to imagine that *Dichterliebe* would not be mentioned as a prime

---

[32] Arnold Whittall, *Musical Composition in the Twentieth Century*, Oxford, Oxford University Press, 1999, 358.

example, and I am equally confident that anyone with an interest in music of the later twentieth century would be likely – really ought – to make a reference to *The Sayings of Péter Bornemisza*.[33] The piano's last postlude in *Dichterliebe* is, rather like Wagner's *Liebestod*, the supreme example, as it were, of its own unique class. Echoes of this postlude can be found scattered throughout music of the next century and a half; it was suggested above (p. 90) that coincidentally it is probably resonating in the closing music of Goehr's *Quadrille*.

In *The Sayings*, based on texts by the eponymous sixteenth-century Hungarian preacher, Kurtág takes Schumann's astonishing 'voice of the piano' to a different plane, into an alienating, chthonic cosmos. Not for nothing does he call this work a 'concerto' for soprano and piano. That is a deliciously ambivalent title, though also a clear reference to Baroque precedents, putting the voice and the piano in a kind of equipoise as we ask ourselves which of these figures is the soloist, and inviting us to muse on the trope of that struggle for attention – not to be *heard* like everyone for 'fifteen minutes' to use Warhol's famous prediction, or in this case at least forty minutes, but to be *listened to* – which unfulfilled need was surely one of the central, Warhol-kitschified crises of late twentieth-century life.

Almost by way of a bagatelle, I want to draw attention – as we sit expectantly waiting for Schumann's poet of love, or Kurtág's priestess of exhortation, to animate their magic landscapes of humanity in the raw, and in its timeless ecstasy – to the *animateurs* (as I see them) of these stories raising their hands to their keyboards. In Schumann's case the famous 7th, the famous opening phrase-repetition:

Ex. 4.6: Schumann, *Dichterliebe,* opening

In Kurtág's case repetition of a different kind,[34] but also the 7th:

[33] Perhaps the most easily accessible recording of *The Sayings* is a 1995 Hungaroton CD, HCD 31290. For a brief guide to Kurtág's life and music, see Péter Halász, *György Kurtág*, Budapest, Magus, 1998.

[34] This opening is discussed in Beatrice Barazzom's article 'Kurtág's Music: The Spectacle of Nature, the Breath of History – from Op. 7 to 27', in *Studia Musicologica*, 43/3–4, 2002, 253–67, 256. See also Rachel Beckles Willson, 'Bulgarian Rhythm and its Disembodiment in *The Sayings of Péter Bornemisza*, Op. 7', in *Studia Musicologica*, 43/3–4, 2002, 269–80.

Ex. 4.7: György Kurtág, *The Sayings of Péter Bornemisza,* Op. 7, opening

Now I am not talking of influence here, or not necessarily so, but after all, in terms of music history we are viewing phenomena that come from pretty much the same stable even if more than a century apart, from the same continental European landscape, and for the same forces, on ecstatic narrative themes, and at what – in their historical contexts – will prove to be monumental length.

In that spirit we shall be looking at one of Kurtág's 'flower' songs, Song 7 of the eight items forming Part 3 of this cycle or 'concerto', the part that carries the overall title 'Death', alongside, Schumann's Song 8 of the sixteen in *Dichterliebe*, 'Und wüssten's die Blumen', known in English as 'And if the Flowers Knew'. Schumann is working against strong background expectations of his audience as to how the form may unfold, whereas one of the important qualities of Kurtág here as elsewhere is that we almost do not know what to expect in any sense, and these different esthesic backdrops need to be borne in mind at all times. 'Und wüssten's die Blumen' is quite surprising in the formal world of 1840, when in this rather short cameo an apparently aggressively strophic, intensely repetitious construction suddenly proliferates not just once in verse 4, especially in its harmonic swerve to the submediant, but twice, when immediately after the brokenhearted voice has given up, in the stunned silence of perhaps unintended personal revelation, the piano launches into six closing bars of unprecedented reverie – unprecedented in the closed world of *Dichterliebe*, although those hearing the wider Schumann here will instantly recognize the flashback to

Ex. 4.8: György Kurtág, *The Sayings of Péter Bornemisza,* Op. 7, Pt 3, No. 7

Ex. 4.8: (*cont.*)

Ex. 4.8: (*cont.*)

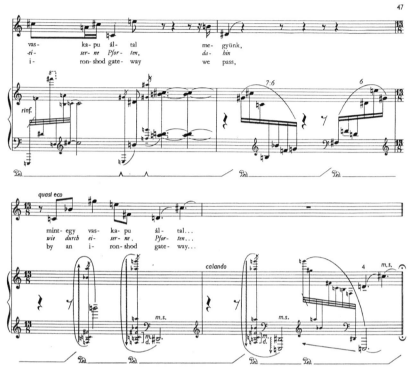

Ex. 4.8: (*cont.*)

the opening of *Kreisleriana*, as the language of the purely instrumental invades Heine's texted space, a point that, oddly, Charles Rosen fails to mention when discussing what he calls the 'startling' and 'unprecedented' phenomenon of this piano coda.[35]

Kurtág's ghastly rather than ghostly text – which it is easy to forget is not a modern one, but centuries older than Heine's – gave him great pause for thought in setting the penultimate number of his 'Death' section, as Rachel Beckles Willson notes from her study of the sketches:

> Just as only through a firmly locked and bolted door
> could we enter a beautifully fragrant, flowering, fruitful garden,
> or a freshly decorated mansion,
> So it is into eternal life through death,
> through the iron gate we go, through the iron gate . . .[36]

[35] Charles Rosen, *The Romantic Generation*, London, HarperCollins, 1996, 210–11.
[36] This translation is taken from Beckles Willson's dissertation; see note 37.

He was concentrating above all on the image of the 'flowers', finally drawing a box around his vocal setting of this word (see score p. 44, third system, bar 2, where the traditional English translation happens to have the word 'blossoming' where the Hungarian word is 'flowers') with the annotation in the holograph copy: 'Let this be the starting point!'[37] But in her account of this song, Beckles Willson rightly has the voice of the piano constantly in mind: 'The time signature of $\frac{10}{8}$', she writes, 'implies something calculated and precise, yet the rapid flow of ornamental figuration' – which I take to mean in the piano – 'operates not to emphasize, but rather to disguise this precision.' And further: 'In the first section, above a sustained bass chord . . . unpedalled, quirky, sparkling figuration sets off resonances in the piano', to which I would add that so, probably, does the voice from bar 3. And further, having noted Kurtág's unusual decision to repeat the words 'through the iron gate' – which appears here on pp. 46 into 47 as 'by an ironshod gateway', that: 'A more evocative sense of parting, of loss, is hard to conceive. Especially touching are the piano's last pitches, echoing those of the voice, reinforcing the absence of one departed by merely repeating the incomplete.'[38] It is this echo that was one of my main reasons for selecting this number – or 'extract' or 'moment' – because it is so overt and unmissable, and raises the question of why this priestess and this piano are in the same arena together.

Meanwhile, let us just consider again that urge to proliferation, as Kurtág works to harness such mighty forces, for him, as his 'concerto' demanded – giving a foretaste of his later proliferation of ways to wrap, or not wrap, the human voice in an extraordinary litany of sound worlds – violin and cimbalom in the Op. 8 'In Memory of a Winter Sunset', chamber ensemble in the Op. 11 'Four Songs', the Op. 17 'Messages of the Late Miss R. V. Troussova' premiered in 1981, the Op. 35 Hölderlin songs; or, for example, violin, double-bass and cimbalom in the Op. 19 'Scenes from a Novel'. And then the other logics: in the recent Opp. 36 and 37, the Beckett and Lichtenberg settings respectively, works to be performed 'with or without instruments'; and thus, of course, the various works, including works-in-progress, for solo voice. Just as Schumann reinvented the Lied he had studied in Beethoven, Schubert, Mendelssohn, and any number of contemporaneous minor composers, and just two decades before Baudelaire was to coin and elucidate the term 'modernity', so we see Kurtág in the 1960s and beyond straining at the boundaries of a new vision of the Lied

---

[37] Rachel Beckles Willson, 'An Analytical Study of György Kurtág's *The Sayings of Péter Bornemisza*, Op. 7 (1963–68)', PhD dissertation, King's College, London, 1998, 160.

[38] Ibid., 158–9.

genre, to some extent via the mediation of Schoenberg's *Das Buch der hängenden Gärten*. And the point of that brief litany is to encourage us to hear something quite settled in 1968; if it is far from being atavistic, nevertheless this is only the beginning of Kurtág's elaborate journey away from the Lied as he inherited it. Like Schumann's Lied-world (and this is a main reason why Roland Barthes was so fascinated by Schumann's songs), Kurtág's is one of intense instrumental extravagance. Stephen Walsh wrote that in *The Sayings* 'taken as a whole, the piano writing uses every resource of the instrument, even at times to the point of over-extending its expressive powers',[39] although I am sure Walsh would be the last to tell us that the quo of the drama is not worth the quid of the extravagance that yields it up.

I have quoted Walsh not because I think he is right, but because it is an interesting case of the point being missed via some instinct for the truth. When the piano, in *Sayings* as in *Dichterliebe*, is an embodiment of expressive intensity, to speak of 'over-extending . . . expressive powers' is but a lame, critical, verbal reflection of a fabulous artistic act of extravagance and proliferation for which I have been trying to find better words here. There is, however, a difference in the *nature* of that intensity, which has nothing to do with 'expressive powers', but everything to do with what is being expressed. For in *Dichterliebe* the piano is in a most special kind of balance with the singer where the 'voice' of one is reflected in and reflects the voice of the other, yet in the end they must live in their own worlds. Hence, I believe, the misguided nature of attempts to regard the end of *Dichterliebe* as any kind of summing-up or even really any kind of 'final' word, since the singer has been left in a different space with *his* final word. We shall find this feature foreshadowed in miniature in Schubert's 'Erster Verlust' in Chapter 5 (see pp. 125–32). Obviously, in Péter Bornemisza's world of confession and revelation, of the agony and the ecstasy of the human being almost as a mere category in God's utterly maddening universe, Kurtág cannot possibly even think of some kind of Schumannian, push-pull complicity between voice and piano. As we have seen by way of one short example, the voice and the hands are, yes, contemplating the same things – hence the many levels of musicostructural intertwinings in the fabric of the music throughout Kurtág's cycle. But one has the feeling that they are not doing it together, so much as just at the same time: alienation on a higher plane.

[39] Walsh, 'György Kurtág: An Outline Study (I)', in *Tempo*, 140, March 1982, 11–21.

The main point I want to make here is that disintegration, heralded by the acute phenomenon of protomodernist 'otherness' posited so timelessly in the Lied landscape by Schumann in 1840 – and that disintegration that explains the integral plot of the 'Sin' part of *The Sayings* – was taken to a level of intensity by Kurtág in Op. 7 that sinks into our awareness of the very medium. Vocality as a medium of disintegration is, then, some kind of opposite of what we found in Brahms's 'Von ewiger Liebe', but it is possible only *because* of the underlying sense that we do make of *The Sayings* as a 'song cycle' for voice and piano with all that that implies as to articulation, contrast and continuity, and dramatic planning. As Whittall comments: 'With an intensity unrivalled in the music of its time . . . the extended sequence of miniatures comprising Bornemisza projects its contrasting yet predominantly black moods in music of extraordinary freedom and focus which, apart from anything else, puts the more textural kind of indeterminate composition of Lutoslawski and Penderecki . . . firmly into the shade.'[40]

MEN FLYING

Breathe again. Whatever else one might think of *Stripsody*, it is refreshing. Just as the austere Schoenberg led us from Chapter 3 into this chapter, so now the exuberance of something quintessentially American, post-1945 American, of the America that had turned popular art into its people's idea of art as capitalist entertainment, provides a backdrop for Copland's bright world to follow in Chapter 5. Cathy Berberian (1928–83) was above all a brilliant singer, with a wide repertoire but a penchant for new music, composed for her by such as Berio, Cage, Pousseur and, most famously (and, history may yet prove, importantly) Stravinsky. *Stripsody* was commissioned for a festival of contemporary music by Bremen Radio in 1966. The graphics are by the Italian cartoonist Roberto Zamarin, best known for his incarnation of the nineteenth-century revolutionary leader Gasparazzo (also depicted in a Vancini film) as a comic-strip character emblematic of the class struggle in post-Fascist Italy. The qualities of *Stripsody* make it a considerable challenge to discuss in the context of intense study of musical scores, for it is not in any generally recognized sense a musical score; it also asks challenging aesthetic questions about what a piece of music, or specifically a 'song', is. For if it is such, then it can only be with a number of caveats for the listener

40 Whittall, *Musical Composition*, 357.

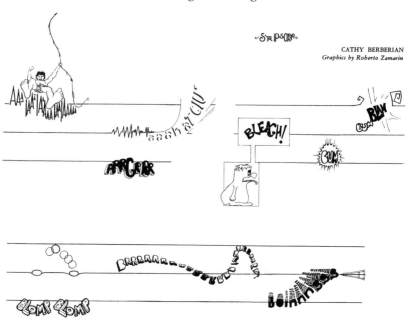

Ex. 4.9: *Stripsody*, p. 1
© 1966 by C F Peters Corporation, New York, reproduced by permission of Peters Edition Limited, London

who might be expecting words, and if not words, then musical 'notes'; if it is a 'song' to the extent that it can be so defined, one will also naturally ask what it is 'about', and that, too, is susceptible to no easy explanation. Let it be said, though, that these deferrals represent positives rather than negatives (unless you are uncomfortable with art of the twentieth-century avant-garde that does not even offer the cultural solace – somewhere we can *place* it – of being largely incomprehensible or at least, in the Bergian sense discussed in Chapter 3 above, 'difficult'). *Stripsody* is entertaining, as surely anyone would agree who is able to appreciate some of its cultural resonances – to appreciate the way we view children in modern Western society, for example, our view of the animals we tend to encounter, or perhaps most overtly our instinct for some of the conventions of mid-century American comic-strip language, sound and gesture.

Ex. 4.9 reproduces the first page of the score of *Stripsody*. Some relevant comments from the brief instructions to the performer need to be assimilated:

The score should be performed as if by a radio sound man, without any props, who must provide all the sound effects with his voice. The three lines represent the different pitch levels: low, medium and high.

The lines enclosed by bars are to be performed as 'scenes' in contrast to the basic material which is a glossary of onomatopoeia used in comic strips.

Whenever possible, gestures and body movements should be simultaneous with the vocal gestures . . .

Basically, the spacing of the 'sound words' indicates the timing.[41]

It almost goes without saying that these instructions are of their time, not least in the reference to the sound 'man' and 'his' voice. They are also, however, a miniature study in performance practice and suggest a high degree of 'learning' on the part of the performer as to:

- precision (pitch 'levels' of the human voice);
- cultural awareness (comic-strip conventions);
- dramatic convention (how to make something a 'scene' through, presumably, not only all the devices of musical articulation available but also bodily gesture and such parts of the acting toolkit as facial expression);
- a sense of timing (to interpret 'spacing' on the score);
- an ability to realize an 'idealized' notation in the sense that iconic items, protowords, or actual words, may be aligned vertically on the three-line systems in the score of *Stripsody*, so that by definition – of one singer with one set of vocal apparatus – these seemingly coincident, aligned objects must always be suggestive of some mode of performance rather than literal instructions to achieve the impossible.

If the effect of all this is what Kramer would mean in this instance by 'just singing' (see Introduction, p. 5), then however instinct-driven and effortless the result may seem to be we can also appreciate that there is a high degree of 'making' going on in a performance of *Stripsody* and in its reception, and not at all incommensurate with the kind of skill and artistry required of performer and listener in the case of 'Von ewiger Liebe' or any of the other music discussed elsewhere in this book.

What the performer needs to know in order to interpret Ex. 4.9 is specifically, for instance, the movie image of Tarzan swinging through the trees (this is what the letter As and the sticks in the first icon must be?) and the sound image of 'aaaah' and so on, which is a particular kind of vocalization Westerners have adopted from films and television as a 'sign' of this situation – the wild and supersimian, expressing both nature in the raw and human transcendence. Secondly, one needs to 'know' the affective state

---

[41] Cathy Berberian, *Stripsody*, New York, Peters, 1966, second page (title page verso).

expressed by the endearing little character in the box in the second 'scene': he (if it is agreed that 'he' looks more male than female or androgynous?), in saying or singing 'Bleagh!' and with that look on his face, whatever it is, is at least not addressing the United States Congress on a complex political issue, or scrubbing up to perform a complex neurosurgical procedure? By the end of this page of icons we are on surer territory, for although the word 'boing' (pronounced 'bɔyng') has yet to make it into the *Oxford English Dictionary*, if it ever does, any English speaker will know that it means the sound that a spring or bell makes or something of the kind; and everyone who has watched Disney animations knows that recursive outlines such as we see here above the bold-text word and around the wedge-shaped object pointing us forward in the piece and over the page represent, clearly (it is not a matter of opinion), vibration, such as may be experienced by a large and often dopey cat hit on the head by a tiny crusading mouse with a huge frying pan. But thirdly, the performer has to be able to reproduce that, somehow. This is remarkably fecund musical terrain, it appears.

It begins (like the musical 'sentence', described by nineteenth-century music theorists as an archetypal Classical thematic construction) with an idea that is immediately followed by a contrasting idea, but one not so unrelated to the first as to compromise the work as a work. Tarzan as depicted here and the 'bleagh'-ing little character in a box inhabit the same kind of cartoon universe; they just play very different roles in it. There follows a transition of material developing the opening: notice, for instance, the various tropes here on the letter, and more importantly in the sound-world, of 'B' and on the interplay of different vowels and diphthongs. The explosive opening seems to have used a fairly full vocal tessitura with two ascents up the register, for even squeaking mice on p. 12 are notated no higher. Then in the second system the tessitura settles around the middle of the range. This is not self-evidently the opening of a 'piece of music' perhaps in its various customary senses, but as a simulacrum of a piece of music, or things like words being made to do something like singing, it is far from being beyond explanation and seems to be anything but wilful in relation to our common ideas of how human communication tends to proceed. Hierarchy is in the wings, too. The second page contains merely a little smudgy drawing and (written in what is obviously, delightfully, a child's writing) 'you stupid kid, come down out of that tree!' with an 'E' and a question mark crossed out at the end of 'tree', and with no pitch-lines or other overt indication of pitch. In Berberian's recorded performance this line is spoken rather than sung or otherwise vocalized. Thus the immediate, foreground contrast of the opening two images (Ex. 4.9) is nested in a larger contrast between what becomes in context the stylistically highly unified first page and the distinct voice and semantic clarity of the second.

I am going to resist an attempt here at any kind of structural analysis of the whole work in a similar manner, not because it cannot be done or would be inordinately long, but because it would probably not be 'true' in the sense of representing poietic intention or likely esthesic response. It is always possible to identify patterns in the ordinary human experience of even the most apparently heterogeneous objects, but it is not always worth while to do so, and especially in a case such as this where the generic and cultural contexts say different.

Generically, *Stripsody* is itemizing from the comic-strip repertory, so that we have, for instance, a breakfast scene on p. 3 if the icons are anything to go by, and they are all we are given – crackling cereal in a bowl, with the words 'crunk', 'crak' and 'crackle', and a thin figure with narrow, strained eyes having GULP written vertically through her (?her) with 'G' as the mouth followed by a fatter figure with GOSH drawn across ?her with 'O' as the mouth, and GULP letters apparently now inside her torso. Then p. 5, top system, offers a cat-and-dog fight, with a wonderfully evil-looking stalking dog ('Sniff Sniff') and a noisy cat who unfortunately – but this is the genre – seems eventually to have been punched completely through the page, leaving the two-dimensional, splatted, cut-out image. There is also on p. 11 a relatively complex cowboy scene, or at least this is in part what is going on; and about halfway through Berberian is not afraid, on p. 8 immediately preceding a weather forecast, to play with icons of Western music including coloratura, a guitar tablature along with the hands playing it, and the Beatles' words 'She's got a ticket to ride'.

Culturally, let us not forget that Berberian as a connoisseur and leading interpreter of American and European composition of the post-Second-World-War avant-garde was fully attuned to new ways of constructing art. Visually, *Stripsody* with or without its comic-strip credentials can stand without the imposition of structural analysis as a collage in the age of collage described by Glenn Watkins;[42] as some kind of reflection of the 1960s idea of a 'happening', although with only the appearance of spontaneity; as an anticipating of the 'installation' that became a catch-all term for multimedia colonizations of late-twentieth-century art galleries. Musically, *Stripsody* is not only a collage, but also subscribes to something of the aesthetic of Stockhausen's idea, one shared with many composers of the period,

---

[42] See for example Glenn Watkins, *Pyramids at the Louvre*, Cambridge, Mass., Harvard University Press, 1994, with his subtitle *Music, Culture, and Collage*.

of 'moment' form, which as Whittall encapsulates the matter 'implies a multivalent and mobile, rather than cumulative or goal-directed, response to the connectivity of a work's materials'.[43]

Nevertheless, even though one can and I believe should argue against structural analysis of 'connectivity' in a work of this kind, it would be insensitive not to record the appearance near the end, 'climactically' it might be said if analytically it must be said, of not a bird, 'no', not a plane, 'no', but 'Superman' – again, with a certainty of reference that simply cannot be lost on any normal member or at least consumer of Anglo-American culture. Unlike Tarzan, Superman never did have a 'cry' or associated vocalization of any kind in the films or on television or in videogames, so in this portrayal Berberian has to settle for verbalization. Superman's appearance, a modern *deus ex machina*, is exquisitely drawn, with binoculars spotting a skeletal bird pierced by an arrow that was previously Cupid's, one can but hope, then a propeller-plane in line drawing seen through some kind of calibrated 'sight' device crossed out, leading to a negative-image Superman in arms, torso and legs, in full-bounding, cloaked pose, right fist raised, with a slight overtone of nudity that may suggest a statue from classical Greece and that in any case stands in rather majestic, refined contrast to the relatively vulgar Tarzan who was heading straight at us large-feet- and fig-leaf-first on p. 1. Because Superman has no associated verbalization, it is not churlish to suggest that his appearance is one of the weaker aspects of *Stripsody*: although the grouping of the words 'bird/plane/Superman' is 'iconic' almost to the point of the subtle irony that I believe Berberian has in mind here, in contextual terms of the wash of vocal variety in this work, of its unanticipated sounds, of its sheer celebration of what the female actress can offer to an audience beyond words and notes, perhaps *Stripsody's* Superman falls a little flat in performance. Even though the situation is rescued with resumed artistry by the closing page, as we shall see, all the same one might observe that artistry perceived as *necessary* may never be the greatest of possible artistry. However that may be, Superman's structural place in *Stripsody* is unquestionable. He and Tarzan are the main characters, the only potential copyright infringers in this wacky world of otherwise more or less anonymous pseudohumans and cute animals. They make for a powerful framing device (see my comments on Goehr's *Quadrille*, p. 92).

Now, nothing would be less welcome to author or reader here or anywhere in these pages than detailed critical griping, which it is hoped has been otherwise avoided altogether, but if the perception that Superman's

---

[43] Whittall, *Musical Composition*, 321.

Ex. 4.10: *Stripsody*, p. 16
© 1966 by C F Peters Corporation, New York, reproduced by permission of Peters Edition Limited, London

appearance in *Stripsody* is, while being of unquestionable structural significance, also something that 'falls a little flat', it is worth mentioning, and
in fact focally, because if it is weak then what makes it weak is a precise
function of its vocality. There *is* no vocal sign, emblem, signal for, representation of, Superman. There appears to be nothing Berberian can sing or
vocalize, nothing she can suggest to other interpreters to sing or vocalize,
that does the work for Superman that is done for Tarzan by 'aaaah' and the
wavy pattern on the middle line signifying that well-known undulating,
almost ululating form of pitch (see Ex. 4.9 – a pattern that also carries connotations, surely, of a sound represented on the screen of an oscilloscope,
possibly also nowadays of other kinds of positive/negative time-mapping
such as a picture of cardiac activity or drawings from the notorious American
'lie detector' device). To put it the other way round, Superman's markedly
unvocalized, basically verbal stage-entrance in *Stripsody* underlines what
was the truly strong vocality of the opening, of which the 'Bleagh!' character's sound-icons and the 'B'-extensions on p. 1 and beyond become comprehensible attenuations and even, at the danger of being 'overanalysed',
developments.

   This reading seems to me confirmed by the end of this work (see the final
page in Ex. 4.10). As semantic references have zoomed in and out of focus

in the course of the work, a potential has been built up between the actual, the 'reality' of comic-strip characters, and the virtual, the vocalizations, including 'protowords' as they were called above, and certainly also in a live performance some of the inevitably more abstract gestures and facial expressions (as opposed, for example, to the drawing on p. 10 of a little girl snuggling up to what may be a cloth, although more worryingly but not necessarily wrongly in this satirical and sometimes a little disturbing work that 'cloth' could well be taken to be a man's striped tie – Berberian specifies in the opening instructions for this that 'the performer places her thumb in her mouth and cups her other hand to her ear').[44] If Superman is an apotheosis of the actual, and the irony of that will not be lost on any reader, then the virtual returns deceptively for one last time in the final moments. Presumably the image as this denouement commences (see above, Ex. 4.10) is a lasso hanging over a word-steer with a head formed by a cowboy-gloved hand. If this is Dadaesque, so without doubt are the 'ZZZ' figures at the beginning of the second system, but the effect of the page as a whole is imbued with the liquid sounds of the end of the Western alphabet (W, Y, Z). Admittedly there is closing kitsch, as the zzz-ing of an unlucky insect is stopped with a 'bang'; but there is also *atmosphere* as a function of sound. If the end of *Stripsody* is, from the point of view of high culture (see Chapter 2, pp. 33–5), as tasteless as the beginning in its semantic reference, nevertheless Berberian is using vocality with just as much right to the claim of subtlety and of the technical integrity of finely crafted art as we find in the coda of any number of Lieder from a hundred years before. Love it or loathe it, it sings.

[44] See note 41.

CHAPTER 5

To Amherst via Vienna

A CURIOUS EARTH

Those who know something about the story of Emily Dickinson's life – and there is rather little to know in terms of adventure, life events and the like – tend to invest their natural reverence in place, time, themes. Amherst is the supposedly idyllic American town that through Dickinson became a shrine to poetry and to biographical mystery. The mid nineteenth century knew of trains and kangaroos,[1] that is, of technology beyond the imagination of any one person and of lands beyond the possibility of normal, individual travel, but not, say, of penicillin or of world war. Looking back at the Romantic world, from which emerged art that has subsequently been as enduringly adored as it was urgently nurtured at the time, we need to sense its smaller frames and gentler reference points despite its disquietingly lurking contemporary trends of displacement and 'chronosis'.[2] And themes – 'topoi' as they have sometimes come to be called in recent musicological discourse – are usually indexed as such in the many books of secondary literature on Dickinson's thus rather self-evidently 'thematic' poetry, themes that are archetypal, recurrent and arch-Romantic preoccupations of this effulgent poet – love, death, journeys and, not least, heaven itself.[3]

'Place' in thinking about Dickinson means not only Amherst but America, and enfolds ideas that have touched the many dozens of composers – mostly ones who in all fairness must be called the minor artists – stimulated creatively by her eerily rhyming (when it does rhyme) 'verse'. Let us not

---

[1] Dickinson commented on herself – or this is how the phrase has been taken – as 'the only kangaroo among the beauty'. See for example K. Keller, *The Only Kangaroo Among the Beauty: Emily Dickinson and America*, Baltimore, Johns Hopkins University Press, 1979.

[2] This nice neologism, originally in French, appears in Jean-Jacques Nattiez's *The Battle of Chronos and Orpheus*, Oxford, Oxford University Press, 2004.

[3] The printed score of the 'Twelve Songs' offers the composer's prefatory comments including: 'The poems centre about no single theme, but they treat of subject matter particularly close to Miss Dickinson: nature, death, life, eternity.' See *Twelve Songs of Emily Dickinson*, New York, Boosey & Hawkes, 1951, no. 17865.

neglect to bear in mind first and foremost that this is American poetry in the English language, and American English of a dense potency that several generations of artists, commentators and many thousands (probably millions) of ordinary readers have rarely found elsewhere in the museum of this language's finest hours; people think of Chaucer and Shakespeare when pondering where Dickinson sits in the aesthetic pantheon, rather than her roughly contemporaneous Romantic poets such as Wordsworth or Keats, say, who for all their greatness are also more moored in their local landscapes. This kind of comment is not made here to evoke some sort of amazement, which Dickinson needs no one's help in doing for her words alone suffice, but to spy a corner of what Aaron Copland will have been thinking about as he sculpted the 'Twelve Songs' for voice and piano in 1949 ready for its premiere the following year, and sculpted intermittently for more than a decade the resulting 'Eight Songs' for voice and orchestra eventually completed in 1970.[4] As an American, this was *his* poet, possessed through place and her language; the great American ideas of nativeness, assimilation, integration, were part of the comfortable toing and froing between nineteenth-century Amherst and twentieth-century New York.[5] When Copland encounters images in Dickinson (as we shall see below in more detail) such as autumn, dress, earth, flocks and ground, it is – I want to emphasize – as much 'place' as any other mechanism of association that summons up for the composer as for many readers of her lines a certain idea (either by direct experience or through observation) of Northern-hemispheric 'weather', of Caucasian 'dress', of what the world may look and feel like, of American sheep, of burial. Those are highly contingent images that could be easily stumbled over ('dress' as in ceremonial option, for example, rather than whatever we choose to wear; 'flocks' of birds or goats, say).[6] It is almost stating the obvious when we remind ourselves that Copland is well 'acclimatized' to Dickinson – despite the distances of a century, a race (Copland was of Jewish extraction), a gender or two (see below), and medium. He was

---

[4] The 'Eight Songs' are a masterpiece of orchestral transcription. If Copland was tempted to vary the basic musical text of his original work, there is no clear sign of this in the orchestral version. He did, of course, excise one-third of the original work; see also note 11.

[5] I am not going to comment here on the other side of this coin, the abject misery – utter cruelty and dire suffering – that are an integral part of the history of human landscapes. A recent account of Dickinson's 'place' in her world is Domhnall Mitchell's *Emily Dickinson: Monarch of Perception*, Amherst, University of Massachusetts Press, 2000, especially the chapter on '"Homeless at Home": The Politics and Poetics of Domestic Space', 44–87. Mitchell notes that 'with the notable exception of feminists, readers have for the most part remained uninterested in the relationship between Dickinson's writing and politics', 81.

[6] 'Shepherd' would rectify any vagueness in the very next line of 'Going to Heaven!', obviously, but I mention this detail, before looking at the poem, to underline the fleeting, momentary stumbling that is, after all, part of the semantic pleasure we gain from encountering, absorbing and rethinking the poetic.

also cautious about such complicit assumptions, in one respect seemingly, and this one can take to be a good sign of self-aware acclimatization: his original, hand-written reference to the work, in the sketches that are three songs short of the eventual opus, was as 'Amherst Days: Nine Poems of Emily Dickinson, set to music by A.C.'; one can only speculate whether Copland was to come to find that putative title 'Amherst Days' altogether too homely, local, tied to place and probably time, parochial – a feeling that seems well-nigh unavoidable in the hindsight of approval of his eventual neutral title.[7]

Time, too, was on his side. Dickinson's language was and still is more or less fresh in the mind, relatively free of archaism, and to some extent, through its vast and varied influences, itself constitutive of modern American English. It is not that many Dickinson lines have found their way into anthologies of quotations (such as 'Parting is all we know of heaven,/And all we need of hell')[8] so much as the way in which Dickinson's mode of expressing herself became a kind of ideal of condensed superstatement – a turn of phrase I use by analogy with 'supersaturated' liquids in the physical world, and by way of contrast with the understatement of which Dickinson can only ever be superficially accused – in a language, American, that to the European English eye and ear is more typically extravagant and given to easy overstatement. And within this time that was on his side, the epoch was right for Copland. Born in 1900, in the generation between that of Schoenberg and Boulez, his reaction to musical Modernism, which he studied not only at home but also in Paris with Nadia Boulanger, was to mediate its extreme urges through the American, the lyrical, the popular. Modernism was something he turned to his advantage as a composer of the 'people' (a 'people' that all the same made his everyday life as a homosexual and alleged communist intermittently extremely challenging), yearning for the kind of homestead security that had been in some sense precisely the bedrock of Dickinson's ability to think and write long and hard in her late 1850s and early 1860s Massachusetts home built originally by her grandparents – whereas Copland, like so many of America's fine creative minds of the twentieth century, was a second-generation immigrant living in the

---

[7] The Dickinson sketches are in the Aaron Copland Collection, Music Division, Library of Congress, Box/Folder 84; they can be viewed on the Library of Congress website, digital ID 'copland sket0032'. The composer notes that he had also considered the titles *Emily's World* (a particularly twee one), *Dickinson Cycle* and *Toward Eternity*. See Aaron Copland and Vivian Perlis, *Copland Since 1943*, New York, St Martin's Press, 1989, 159.

[8] From No. 1732, 'My life closed twice before its close'. (Most of Dickinson's known poems are usually referred to by their 'Johnson' numbers. See for example *Emily Dickinson: The Complete Poems*, ed. T. Johnson, London, Faber, 1975 (first paperback edition) for a readily available source). 'Going to Heaven' and other subsequent quotations from Dickinson poems are from this edition.

diaspora that bears their deep imprimatur to this day. Such approximate synchronicity is alive, too, in the 'time' of Romanticism; for in his rekindling of musical tradition (Copland's 'Going to Heaven!' uses, for example, to look for the obvious, conventional reprise and variation techniques) this composer is in touch with just the kind of structuration that literary critics also find as an anchor in Dickinson. Cristanne Miller notes that 'Dickinson lived in a century that adored repetition in almost every form: think of the incantatory verbal and aural repetitions of Poe's poetry, the enormous prestige and popularity of orators like Daniel Webster, the Wagnerian leitmotive. It would be strange if Dickinson, in this context, did not structure her poetry through various repetitions.'[9]

As to themes, Copland, like many other composers, could hardly fail to be drawn to Dickinson's extraordinary combination of interiority and experience. The former quality we shall come to in a poem about afterdeath that turns to its completely-taken-aback reader in line 11, saying out of the blue, 'Perhaps you're going too!', like a conversation over tea switching suddenly to the infinities of what we can barely take in. But the experience, too, is a lovely ride for the composer. One need think only of Dickinson's joy in telling us, with her customary word here and little phrase there, of fantastic journeys, this one being the last, we imagine, or as far as we can imagine, but matched in Dickinson's poems of living with a whirlwind of 'going to Kansas, up Alps, across deserts, through jungles . . . off to sea',[10] just all over the world, 'such a curious earth' that she does mention in 'Going to Heaven!' – which it is time now to read:

> **Going to Heaven!**
> Going to Heaven!
> I don't know when,
> Pray do not ask me how, –
> Indeed, I'm too astonished
> To think of answering you!   5
> Going to heaven! –
> How dim it sounds!
> And yet it will be done
> As sure as flocks go home at night
> Unto the shepherd's arm!   10
>
> Perhaps you're going too!
> Who knows?

[9] Cristanne Miller, *Emily Dickinson: A Poet's Grammar*, Cambridge, Mass., Harvard University Press, 1987, 75.

[10] Jane Donahue Eberwein, *Dickinson: Strategies of Limitation*, Amherst, University of Massachusetts Press, 1985, 109.

If you should get there first,
Save just a little place for me
Close to the two I lost!   15
The smallest "robe" will fit me,
And just a bit of "crown";
For you know we do not mind our dress
When we are going home.

I'm glad I don't believe it,   20
For it would stop my breath,
And I'd like to look a little more
At such a curious earth!
I am glad they did believe it
Whom I have never found   25
Since the mighty autumn afternoon
I left them in the ground.

Copland left this poem pretty much untouched, including repetitions the significance of which it is likely that detailed analysis will always tend to exaggerate – the fact that Copland repeats 'going to heaven' various times, including at the opening, is almost neither here nor there; it is a token, were one needed, of how in song words often need to have special attention drawn to them if the composer wants us to 'hear' them with semantic resonance.[11] Given that, he has come up with an inspired motif for this phrase:

---

[11] One may suspect that it is just such 'semantic resonance' that led Copland to withdraw Song 3 of the 'Twelve' from the 'Eight'. It is a particularly dignified, touching composition that surely deserves its place in the original cycle. However, as his notion of cyclicity matured even further, I imagine – that is, speculate – that Copland came to see how these sweet sentiments (quoted with original punctuation, then unknown to Copland, from Johnson, *The Complete Poems*, No. 249, 113–14):

> Why – do they shut me out of Heaven?
> Did I sing – too loud?
> But – I can say a little 'Minor'
> Timid as a Bird!
>
> Wouldn't the Angels try me –
> Just – once – more –
> Just – see – if I troubled them –
> But don't – shut the door!
>
> Oh, if I – were the Gentleman
> In the 'White Robe' –
> And they – were the little hand – that knocked –
> Could – I – forbid?

had to be sacrificed in favour of 'Going to Heaven!'. The movement from exclusion to ecstatic anticipation creates what he perhaps came to see as an unwarranted, distracting subplot implicating Songs 3 and 11 together from the 1950 work.

Ex. 5.1: Vocal opening of 'Going to Heaven!'
© Copyright 1951 by the Aaron Copland Fund for Music, Inc., copyright renewed.
Boosey & Hawkes, Inc., sole licensee.

It will stand a great deal of reiteration, although its final instrumental setting at the tritone (B flat) against the singer's closing tonal 'ground' (E) is as unexpected as it is poignant – and poetically decisive – in ways that will be discussed below.[12] In general his response to the poem is a spirited one, moving from excitement[13] to the closing speculative mood: the mode is persistently major, as are most of the individual harmonies; there is even a hint of the 'pastoral' (an 'affect' that is never far away in any brisk, major-mode music in $\frac{6}{8}$ time) to see the 'flocks . . . home'. One good reason for taking Copland's reading as amounting to 'a lovely ride' – to take one small lateral look here – is our knowledge of his preoccupation with 'The Chariot', which became the final song of the twelve (and the later eight):

---

[12] I am not aware that anyone has traced a source for this motive, if there is one, although it was once suggested to me by a Dickinson scholar that it is strongly reminiscent of the mid-twentieth-century guard's sing-song announcement on the Philadelphia railway out of New York.

[13] Copland notes in a letter to the composer Irving Fine of 10 March 1950, perhaps before he had fixed the precise order of the twelve songs: 'The Dickinson cycle is done except for a fast song [perhaps Song 6, 'Dear March, come in!] in the middle. (Why didn't you tell me *fast songs are hard to write*?)', See Library of Congress, the Aaron Copland Collection, digital ID 'copland corr0614' (my emphasis).

Originally I had no intention of composing a song cycle using Emily Dickinson's poems. I fell in love with one poem, 'The Chariot'. Its first lines absolutely threw me . . . After I set that poem, I continued reading Emily Dickinson. The more I read, the more her vulnerability and loneliness touched me. The poems seemed the work of a sensitive yet independent soul. I found another poem to set, then one more, and yet another. They accumulated gradually.[14]

The title of Dickinson's poem about a carriage journey with death is not authentic, but the opening lines are perhaps among the very best known of hers, 'Because I could not stop for Death – / He kindly stopped for me – '. It was a momentous journey on to which Copland had latched, as 'we', she and Death, 'slowly drove'; 'we passed the School . . . the Fields of Gazing Grain . . . the Setting Sun', and eventually Dickinson tells us that this was centuries ago, if feeling like a 'Day' fresh from her own life when she had 'first surmised the Horses' Heads/ Were toward Eternity – '.

It is possible, right even, to contemplate the seriousness of such themes, and Dickinson critique is replete with earnest discussion of such matters. 'Going to Heaven!', when it is mentioned specifically, tends to generate responses concerning theology and tropes. Theology is found, for example, in lines 20–1 (about being glad not to believe it – the going to heaven – for it would stop her breath) where the speaker is said to reveal 'her pronounced negative attitude towards images of an after-life as offered by Christian doctrine. Her strong revocation is embedded in a positive feeling that is nurtured by her full acknowledgement of man's finitude. The notion that death might not be the end of existence makes her suffocate.'[15] This last comment perhaps misses Dickinson's touch of a certain macabre and deeply humanizing – sensitizing – humour ('it would' indeed 'stop my breath'), although Paula Bennett is undoubtedly correct to say that this poem is among those that 'confirm Dickinson's religious links to her period', and even though she finds this particular 'early' text 'highly sentimental'.[16]

The tropes of heaven and home in particular are discussed extensively in Dickinson reception-literature. Sometimes this is a coolly analytical matter, as when James Guthrie finds 'Going to Heaven!' to be a good example for his general, persuasive view that 'Dickinson had to stipulate two contradictory requirements for heaven: it had to be familiar enough to be

---

[14] Copland and Perlis, *Copland Since 1943*, 158.

[15] Katharina Ernst, *'Death' in the Poetry of Emily Dickinson*, Heidelberg, Carl Winter Universitätsverlag, 1992, 112–13.

[16] Paula Bennett, *Emily Dickinson: Woman Poet*, Hemel Hempstead, Harvester Wheatsheaf, 1990, 59. The dating of Dickinson's poems, in this case about 1859, is in nearly all cases a matter of inference and conjecture.

comfortable, yet different enough to inspire awe'.[17] On the other hand, a psychoanalytical approach offers more challenges to our ability to assimilate the interpretation, as when John Cody notes that ' "home" may be equivalent to "heaven" in the conventional religious sense', but heaven itself is a crucially mediated idea: 'If the concept of heaven had any validity at all for Emily Dickinson, it conveyed a state in which severed relationships could be re-established and rendered permanently secure. Her constant dreaming of her father indicates how unready she was to part with him and suggests the extent of her need to preserve him alive within her.'[18] The death of her father did not occur until 1874, when Dickinson had already written about two-thirds of her poems, and long after this one; but Cody's psychological point is not undermined in what it says about her attitude, and the claimed utilitarian appropriation of the after-life is inferred, too, by Paul Ferlazzo from his reading of this particular poem, a reading that stands sharply aside from the partisan championing often and understandably to be found in the literature on her poetry.

Again, chronology is not so important, in that a 'sense of worry about salvation after death takes many forms in every period of her life'. Ferlazzo says that the poem 'begins in orthodoxy' – although that might be thought a strange implication of opening lines that begin with such acute apposition of the supposedly known (supposed because, after all, who says there is a heaven, and if there is, that we can go there?) and the supposedly unknown (not knowing 'when' – which surely invites us to think beyond some tedious speculation on a mortal illness, suicidal intention, or the anticipation of any dangerous situation, and so Dickinson is telling us implicitly how well the poet feels in the poetic now of life). By the end of line 9, though, Dickinson has distorted 'the conventional images of the afterlife to end in blatant skepticism'. Ferlazzo believes that the second stanza begins 'sardonically', as well as 'impishly', asking the reader to save a place for her (some might find Dickinson's 'If you should get there first' much more than sardonic or impish, but a dire warning to anyone, not preoccupied with death, who may need to be reminded of it). She 'separates herself sharply', he says, 'from the conventionally faithful persons', telling us what she does not believe and being glad about not believing it (again a corrective is in order here

[17] James Guthrie, *Emily Dickinson's Vision: Illness and Identity in Her Poetry*, Gainesville, University Press of Florida, 1998, 81, in the tellingly entitled chapter 'Poetry as Place: Heaven, Ill/locality, and Continents of Light'.

[18] John Cody, *After Great Pain: The Inner Life of Emily Dickinson*, Cambridge, Mass., Harvard University Press, 1971, 135 and 91 respectively.

from those who intuit that Dickinson is telling *herself* she doesn't believe it, recoiling from its ghastly truth, from the plain fact that death does, and as just mentioned, stop the breath). 'Contemplation of heaven for the faithful', we are then told, 'is reassuring' (is it?), although faith's *seeking* of reassurance is undeniable; 'but for Dickinson, who loves this "curious earth", it is an interference',[19] while also, it must be remembered, being a continual thread in her life's solitary work.[20]

Such theologies and tropes seem to inhabit a different critical space than the lyrical one to be gleaned from Copland's setting, one that would aim rather to capture a special moment of time that takes us on a fantastical ride arriving at the meditative (I am distinguishing this from the 'pensive' mentioned in Chapter 4, p. 93, since it is Copland's *musical* ending using a special *musical* device that seems to be at a premium here). As we saw, Copland wrote of Dickinson's 'vulnerability and loneliness . . . the work of a sensitive yet independent soul'. We have to allow him his romanticized view of the sage of Amherst. He would have been intrigued, presumably, to read Camille Paglia's views on this 'greatest of women poets':

Less melodious than Sappho, Dickinson is conceptually vaster, for she assimilates two more millennia of western experience. No major figure in literary history has been more misunderstood. Ignored by her own time, Dickinson was sentimentalised in her renascence . . . The horrifying and ruthless in her are tempered or suppressed. Emily Dickinson is the female Sade, and her poems are the prison dreams of a self-incarcerated, sadomasochistic imaginist. When she is rescued from American Studies departments and juxtaposed with Dante and Baudelaire, her barbarities and diabolical acts of will become glaringly apparent . . . The primary qualities of Dickinson's style are high condensation and riddling ellipsis . . . Words are rammed into lines with such force that syntax shatters and collapses into itself. The relation of form to content is aggressive and draconian . . . The brutality of this belle of Amherst would stop a truck. She is a virtuoso of sadomasochistic surrealism.[21]

Tough talk, but Paglia's whole chapter on 'Amherst's Madame de Sade'[22] is rich with careful critique and illustration, evidence-based and open to disqualification if her reader wishes, unpersuaded as one might be by the perhaps hyperbolic, and surely stark diagnoses of such characteristics

---

[19] Paul Ferlazzo, *Emily Dickinson*, Boston, Twayne, 1976, 33–4.

[20] For a recent account of Dickinson's need for solitude, see Adam Phillips, *Houdini's Box: On the Arts of Escape*, London, Faber, 2001, 151–7.

[21] Camille Paglia, *Sexual Personae: Art and Decadence from Nefertiti to Emily Dickinson*, New Haven, Yale University Press, 1990, 624.

[22] Ibid., 623–73.

as 'voyeurism, vampirism, necrophilia, lesbianism, sadomasochism, sexual surrealism'.[23] The reader looking out for a corrective to Copland's apparently benign 'view' of Dickinson will certainly find it in Paglia's lurid retellings.

AN EARLIER TIME

Thinking, though, about that 'romanticized view of the sage of Amherst' that has been said here to be found in Copland – a view that I shall indicate can nevertheless be interpreted as, at the very least, also compositionally lucid and honest in terms of the musical work of art – perhaps inevitably leads us into wondering how long is the shadow cast by the great Romantic Lied composers in Copland's mind, and in our reception of his work. Certainly in 1950 Copland himself was, it so happens, in a place of significant personal and compositional transition. Howard Pollack describes the situation in this way:

In the larger context of his career, the *Dickinson Songs* can be seen as part of a trend away from public statements toward more private ones; in some contrast to his earlier work, his postwar music seems more preoccupied with personal . . . issues . . . Such tendencies appear related as well to his adoption of the twelve-tone method in the Piano Quartet, which was composed in tandem with the *Dickinson Songs*. In discussing these two works of 1950, Copland himself alluded to a shift of some sort, writing, 'I have always had an aversion to repeating myself.'[24]

Both before and after this shift, Copland was steeped in the European tradition, and as he himself wrote, completely 'without fear of exhausting the value of the generalized mould'.[25] With his exquisite taste for American popular music – not least as absorbed into his film scores, of which the last for Hollywood, *The Heiress*, had been released only one year before the 'Twelve Songs' – Copland was not only aware of the continuity of the Western, 'classical' lyrical tradition in this overwhelmingly significant, modern, transatlantic, hummed and whistled manifestation,[26] but he was recurrently conscious of his own role within that tradition; even self-conscious, it can be inferred. For these and other obvious music-historical reasons, it makes every kind of sense to consider an earlier 'model' from a different

---

[23] Ibid. 673.

[24] Howard Pollack, *Aaron Copland: The Life and Work of an Uncommon Man*, London, Faber, 2000, 439–40.

[25] Aaron Copland, *Music and Imagination*, Cambridge, Mass., Harvard University Press, 1952, 65.

[26] Lest the reader think this a capricious formulation, I mention that Schoenberg had toyed with the much-quoted wish that people might whistle his tunes.

place and time – the Vienna of Franz Schubert – that all the same is virtually next door and the day before from our perspective. Not the least of those reasons, one that tends towards the music-analytical aspect of critical interpretation, is another 'grammatical' phenomenon of words made to sing, further to our consideration of the 'interrogative' in Chapter 2 – here time, *tense*, the past of the poetic present and the present of the poetic future.

This phenomenon of poeticomusical time seems to me to be one of the noumenal quicks – *the* free-floating substance – of Schubert's Goethe song 'Erster Verlust', 'First Loss'.[27] The interplay of times here, of past, present and future and their interlacings (such as, for example, grammatically, things *going to have been* remembered) decisively transcends 'word-painting', however charming word-painting may be, however imaginative and unforeseen.[28] It does so at a level where words and music unite (though not overlap precisely, as we shall see) in a poetic otherworldliness that is going to bring us back to Copland's twentieth-century 'heaven', which also has its bitingly divergent time-worlds. In 'First Loss' the interplay among tenses and implied tenses is, of course, initially of Goethe's doing rather than Schubert's:

Erster Verlust
'**First Loss**'
Ach, wer bringt die schönen Tage,
Ah, who (can) bring the beautiful days,
Jene Tage der ersten Liebe,
Those days of first love,
Ach, wer bringt nur eine Stunde
Ah, who (can) bring even one hour
Jener holden Zeit zurück!
Of that lovely time back!

[27] Lawrence Kramer has written about this song at least twice, firstly in 'Performance and Social Meaning in the Lied: Schubert's Erster Verlust', in *Current Musicology*, 56, 1994, 5–23; and secondly in *Franz Schubert: Sexuality, Subjectivity, Song*, Cambridge, Cambridge University Press, 1998, Chapter 1, 'Interpretive Dramaturgy and Social Drama: Schubert's "Erster Verlust"', 9–26. His agendas are at best tangential to the points made here.

[28] Reflecting one of the preoccupations of what was for him recent poetry, Schubert seems drawn again and again to elaborations on temporality of one form and another. 'First Loss' does seem rather special in this respect, although one might with justification say that temporality on such a huge canvas as that of Schubert's *Winterreise* song cycle is somehow even more special. An example of a short Schubert song dealing with similar issues but shorn of the love and (explicit) loss is 'Nacht und Träume', D. 827, on a poem by Matthäus von Collin, of which a 'textbook' analysis, available only in German, can be found in Diether de la Motte, *Musikalische Analyse, mit kritischen Anmerkungen von Carl Dahlhaus*, Cassel, Bärenreiter, 1968, 61–71. Although de la Motte offers this as an example of 'Analysis of a Words-and-Music Work' ('*Analyse einer Wort-Ton-Composition*'), his assimilation of the poetry into his critical interpretation of the song is rudimentary and superficial, albeit perhaps appropriate for its intention within his book.

Einsam nähr ich meine Wunde,   5
Alone I feed my wound,
Und mit stets erneuter Klage
And with ever renewed lament,
Traur ich ums verlorne Glück.
I mourn my lost happiness.
Ach, wer bringt die schönen Tage,
Ah, who (can) bring the beautiful days,
Jene holde Zeit zurück!
That lovely time back![29]

No penetrating exercise of textual criticism is needed to assert that Goethe is referring from the present to the past in lines 1–4, and to the present and implied future in lines 5–7 before the varied, contracted repetition in lines 8–9 of the first quatrain. This 'present' tense, however, is one that refers to the future, by asking who is going to be able to bring the past back (it is not here now, so our 'who?' could only be in some future, compared with say the 'real', present '*Wer?*' in the opening words of Goethe's *Erlkönig* in 'The Erlking' – 'Who is riding so late through night and wind?').

In the unlikely event that the reader fails to negotiate this saturated temporality of the one who is experiencing a first loss (loss of beautiful days, of first love, of happiness), the words will in any case fall into themselves with clinical acuity. An interior bargain is struck, so typically of the internal monologue of human misery, although in this case foregrounding chronological technicalities, neuroses perhaps. Say, then – so the prospective deal (with fate?) goes, and to be more specific – that someone could bring back just one *hour*, an hour of that *time*, a time that has been first measured in *days*; it is the desperate chronological quantification of the imprecatory plea-bargain. And 'I feed my wound' gathers up the tenses: the I, now; the feeding – lamenting – going on into the future; the wound that arose, however recently (although it may after all not be such a fresh wound?), in a former time, one that carries a strong scent of epically distant irretrievability, such is the terse conviction in this vignette of nonnegotiable loss-gone-by.

The collusion of tenses carries on, as our scanning for meaning spreads forwards and backwards through the text, even to the austere title 'First Loss', which we may tend to have taken to be inflected as in common parlance – a loss that is the *first* one – when the poem as a whole will leave us contemplating not only the shock of the new (of what is experienced for

---

[29] This is my literal translation designed to map into the German as far as possible without stretching linguistic credulity.

the first time) but also, and perhaps more fundamentally and enduringly in the afterglow of our understanding of this poem, contemplating the straightforwardly and asynchronically grim finitude of loss – loss then, loss now, loss whenever, loss as loss itself. If this final interpretive trope is accepted, it seems that Goethe has been creating out of time timelessness; or in the ludic spirit of the tense-play here we might say that he *has been wanting* us to do so. The lament is a futile narrative in poetic 'reality' in that it cannot do anything at all to rectify the loss, a loss that has happened and has become an eternal fact; lament can, though, do something about the person, who is struggling to place this atemporal wound in an experiential matrix that can be assimilated chronologically in memory and anticipation. And one thing the person can very well do in such trying circumstances is to sing about them.

Admittedly the text of Goethe's words alone can take us only so far in exploring the folds of Schubert's 'Loss'. Theodor Adorno reminded his readers forcefully in his 1928 essay marking the centenary of Schubert's death not to overvalue the premusical in Schubert's vocal music, even taking a nip out of the composer's halo over the issue of text selection, but only to emphasize how relatively important that is: 'his habit of blindly choosing mythological poems, and without making much of a distinction between Goethe and Mayrhofer, is the most dramatic indication of *the uselessness of words in this deep place where poems offer nothing but the materials*'.[30] And my comments above about time in this poem are undoubtedly 'spun' by Schubert's rather clear 'reading' of the text as enshrined in his incantatory, short, but larger-than-life song. These readings, Schubert's as enshrined in the composition itself and the one offered above in supplementary commentary, are essentially the same even if he were to have given no actual thought to the temporality swings.[31] One can say that whatever Goethe's symbolic paradigms may be or may represent, whatever the tags one may give them or different colours, say, in which one could mark them, or different print for 'present' and '*past*', the paradigms are closely reflected in Schubert's song:

[30] Theoder Adorno, 'Schubert', in *Gesammelte Schriften*, vol. xvii, Frankfurt, Suhrkamp, 1997, my translation, my emphasis. Johann Mayrhofer was a close friend of Schubert, a gloomy poet, and a profoundly influential figure in the composer's life, but not one whose reputation survived in Adorno's or anyone else's pantheon of literary greatness. For a brief biography of Mayrhofer, see John Reed, *Schubert (The Master Musicians)*, London, Dent, 1987, 243.

[31] What it might really mean, really imply in respect of our understanding, for a composer to have 'thought' about something remains unclear in most cases, despite the casual and in my view confusing assumptions about compositional intention to be found in so much critical writing on music.

Ex. 5.2: Schubert, 'Erster Verlust', complete, with Schenker overlay

Ah, who (can) bring **the beautiful days**,
Those days of first love,
Ah, who (can) bring **even one hour**
Of that lovely time back!
Alone I feed my wound,
And with ever renewed lament,
I mourn my lost happiness.
Ah, who (can) bring **the beautiful days**,
That lovely time back!

Most importantly, at the underlying harmonic level there is modal interplay in the music, where we can take the minor to exist in the musical present and the major in the past. This may seem a somewhat crude procedure of Schubert's in being so self-evident, even if it has the virtue of coming directly to the attention of any acclimatized listener; yet however that may be, it is a procedure here of astonishing subtlety in that, for instance, Schubert spreads these distinct pigments all over the tonality of the entire musical plot. Does this music or does it not – the reader will have to decide at some stage of 'knowing' this song, or always continue asking – begin 'in' F minor? F minor is the tonality that is asserted not only expressively at the opening, but structurally by the IV – I – V middle section (bars 10–16), which is a classic example of a structural 'interruption', to use Schenkerian terminology, confirming the 'dividing' dominant at the words 'lost happiness' leading to the tonic (F minor) reprise that initiates the closing phrase. Only the last bar is needed to confirm that the tonic is F minor. F minor is a seriously compromised tonic, however.[32] Repeatedly the music treats this tonic as the submediant of its relative major, of the A flat (major) 'tonic' that signals the past in this wistful world of destabilized chronology, providing through a half-cadence the goal of the first phrase at bar 5, and through a full cadence the goal of the first half of the song at bar 9. The singer does truly end in A flat major (bar 21), finally placed by Schubert in the resummoned, major-mode past, in nostalgia and, as it may seem to be to some listeners, in delusion.[33]

---

[32] It is intriguing to perform this song, live with all the cogency that real-time, real-presence performance carries, to a musician-audience that largely does not know it (as many music students will understandably tend not to, for example), simply omitting the last bar. The experience seems to be of something different, not something wrong. See below for further comment on this bar and how Schubert revised it.

[33] I acknowledge the interesting question, asked by Jim Samson at a presentation of some of my work on this song, whether there is anything deliberate, or typical, in Schubert allotting this specific 'time' or mood to minor and that to major, other than the well-known phenomenon in Schubert's music in general of frequent interplay between major and minor modes of the same key. If there is an answer to that question in the Schubert literature, or at least an informed opinion, I have been

I am not saying that Schubert is mapping Goethe's temporality precisely, at least not if it is accepted that the poem in its verbal version deals in *three* species of time, for it would seem to be overinterpreting to find some abstruse musical importation by Schubert of Goethe's 'future' time, an effect that is already in the verbal version a somewhat occluded one – Goethe does not use the future tense as such, or really clearly refer to the future or indeed need to, one might say, since the future is built into the very narrative unfolding of the work of art, be it poem or music. That Schubert is mapping profoundly in two dimensions if not three is certainly claimed here, however, and not least because this mapping takes place also through the very structuring of the song's own time as its story and its music unfold. Although this is evident in various different dimensions of the music, it seems especially clear in the temporal proportions. The 'perceived' time taken by the various phases of the song is a matter of individual response, to some extent, but the periodicity built into the metrical disposition of the components – which one can ascertain simply by agreeing on the significant points of articulation and, to put it baldly, counting up how many bars the components take up – is a reliable indication of one intersubjectively, almost objectively 'true' aspect of the form within this composition:

$$\underline{3+\mathbf{2}+\mathbf{2}+\mathbf{2}} \quad / \quad \underline{3+{}^{*}2+2} \quad / \quad \underline{3+(\mathbf{2})} = 3!$$
$$\underline{= 5+\mathbf{4}}$$
$$9 \quad + \quad 7 \quad + \quad (5) = \mathbf{6}\,!$$

It takes a certain degree of calculation – or call it a special kind of inspiration if the idea of compositional 'calculation' is any kind of obstacle to appreciating the work that Schubert did – to write a song in phrases of 9, 7 and 6 bars (a 6 that, as the diagram above wants to imply, functions as an extended 5).[34] If the italics marked in the bar-groupings above self-evidently reflect, once again here, poetic reference to the past, one might then ask what the apparently four-square *2 + 2 bars are doing in the lamenting present at the middle of the song? But it is that 2 + 2 analysis that is 'wrong' (because of its monodimensional crudity that is so typical of superficial formal analysis

---

unable to find it. It is known, of course, from the research literature that associations of, say, the 'sad' with minor and the 'happy' with major have changed with the passage of time – Schumann, for instance, famously wrote of the positive feelings evoked by the first movement of Mozart's G minor Symphony.

[34] Brian Newbould comments on this proportional structure, in a brief, subtle account of 'this gem of a song' that also mentions the tonal dualism representing recollection and the present, in *Schubert: The Music and the Man*, London, Gollancz, 1997, 51–2. For lack of space, possibly, Newbould did not venture into the one further level of detail – is there an even number of bars in the middle? – that my own brief account here shows to be the essential analytical step.

in general), and not Schubert's handling of the proportions; 'wrong' in the sense that Schubert is listening to a deeper level of articulation, as is only to be expected in such a finely wrought intaglio of a piece that has to be turned over repeatedly under the closest gaze for it to yield its less obvious secrets – here the fact that there are three components of overlapped **three**-bar groupings, multiparametrically, the first articulated by the vocal phrasing, the second by the emergence of a distinct melody in the piano, and the third by the harmonic arrival at the structural dominant. In other words, the seven bars are knitted together as 1ˢᵗ to 3ʳᵈ, 3ʳᵈ to 5ᵗʰ, 5ᵗʰ to 7ᵗʰ:

Bars   10   11   12   13   14   15   16

tune   _____

                         piano's voice____

                                  F minor_____

If the 'voice' of the piano has needed to emerge at this point of the account, in the song this feature has been simmering from the beginning, providing, for instance, the E flat – E – F motif (bars 2–3, bass) that is going to link the first two subphrases (bars 5–6, bass), be imitated in the voice (bar 7) as we realize that it potentially signalled the golden 'hour' now compacted into one bar of piquant chromatic sweetness, inverted in the 'lonely' piano (bars 11–12, 'bass') that is in truth left texturally isolated now as a solo line, and that is built into the retransition back to the tonic (bars 13–17), which, significantly, covers the final two bars – the E flat accompanying the voice left in its dream world of the past (bar 21) now led by the piano through E to F at the close. As the Schubert *Gesamtausgabe* (collected edition) shows, that close in the piano was originally a version of the block chords from the penultimate bar:

Ex. 5.3: Schubert, original version of final bar

With the revision, Schubert is letting the piano 'sing' the voice's cadential quaver motif, heightening through stark antithesis (contradicting like with like) the eloquence, brusque if not brutal, with which the piano drags the song – its listeners anyway – into the gruesome present of everlasting loss through a mere sprinkle of notes: making notes sing.[35]

---

[35] For an exceptionally persuasive and graceful account of another Schubert song revision, innocently free of the pseudopsychoanalytical jargon that was to dog so much of this kind of 'New Musicology' in

'First Loss' is, then, a model of how poetic time can be adapted to musicopoetic time; of taut, transvocal structure; of a general compositional austerity. Compared with the 'big' Schubert song-canvases, all is concentration here. Structurally, it is precisely the kind of art that in general – and I am certainly not saying there was a specific influence – forms the inheritances, the genetic pool, at work in Copland. But more than that, it is also a classic of the truths Schubert was to hand on to song composers of the future. No commentator seems to have captured Schubert's quiddity in this respect better than Adorno, who intends to tell us what such offerings are really about:

> Brook, mill and black winter wastes, expanding in the *Nebensonnen* twilight, as in a dream, outside time – these are the signs of Schubert's landscape, dried flowers are its mournful bloom; the objective symbols of death trigger the images, and the feeling of those images reinforces the symbols of death. There you have the Schubertian dialectic: it absorbs with all the force of subjective interiority the fading images of an objective presence in order to rediscover them in the smallest cells of any musical realization.[36]

Time, mourning, symbol; the fading images of life captured in the enduring essences of music. Adorno sketches with his customary astonishingly concentrated insight the kind of artistic nurture that passes from Vienna to New York, from German to English, from the Enlightened to the Modern, from lament to fantasy.

TO HEAVEN

Schubert's poet is lamenting. We have seen that Copland's is certainly not. Her message is a complex, even – one might want to accept – a muddled one, not in the least muddled in its poetic expression but somehow so in the helter-skelter states of mind it summons with such delicate acuity, and perhaps a little alarmingly. 'Going to Heaven!' is almost certainly – for most readers and listeners, anyway – not about something so absolute and in that pure and uncluttered sense something so 'Enlightened' as lost human love. Goethe had exulted in concise and compact elaboration around a monadic theme that found no place for jagged rhetorical tropes, for scenic 'props' lending dramatic impact or local colour, for any kind of narrative ducking and weaving around the central 'message' of the poem. In contrast,

the 1980s and 1990s, see 'Schubert's Second Thoughts', about the song 'Wasserflut' from *Winterreise*, in Victor Zuckerkandl, *Man the Musician: Sound and Symbol, Volume Two*, Princeton, Princeton University Press, 1976 [1973], 303–12.
[36] Ibid., 24.

'Going to Heaven!' darts between persons (a typically, teasingly obscure 'I', a definitive yet completely unknown 'you'), between places (heaven, home, 'a little place', earth, ground), between times (possible futures and vague pasts, decisive prediction of 'it will be done' and clear memory of 'the mighty autumn afternoon', and perhaps most acutely the modernistically obviated present – 'I'm glad I don't believe it'); it darts between props of sheep, sacred symbols and implied human bodies, between the 'astonished' and the 'dim', the momentous and the 'smallest', the 'sure' and the 'Perhaps'. What is more, one would probably oversimplify even to imply, let alone assert, that it is only straightforward antimonies that are in play here, however multifarious they may be; for the poem alone, regardless of Copland's richly fantastical music that nevertheless shares in something of a Schubertian power of compression, is anything other than inherently dualistic, even though its network of associations necessarily relies on antithesis.

'Going to Heaven!' does tell us plainly, however, of a journey of sorts; of this there can be no doubt. The text offers its 'Going' intently, as is Dickinson's wont with her terse first lines and Romantic repetitions,[37] and it would be difficult to envisage any worthwhile understanding of Copland's setting that were to set its face against this aspect, against the idea of a song of motion, motion in some combination of time, place, experience. The underlying musical 'motion' is either remarkable aesthetically, or historically predictable, depending on your point of view.

As to the latter, any musician nowadays knows perfectly well that to move a piece of music from one tonality to an ending in the tonality at a tritone's distance (in this case B flat major to E major) is as far theoretically as major-minor harmony can be stretched across the circle of fifths, while such a relationship also represents a high degree of affinity.[38] Not only might we find the harmonic 'mould'[39] of this composition predictable, what with all we know about tritonal key relationships, but there has been plenty of local compositional inflection in Copland's setting to herald this overall tonal strategy. In particular, he often uses the upper tritone, a semitone below the dominant note, to fill out the space between the tonic and dominant of a major triad – hence, for example, the Ds in a prolonged accompanying A flat major triad from bar 20, Cs in a similar G flat major triad from bar 30,

---

[37] See Miller, *Emily Dickinson: A Poet's Grammar*.

[38] In Bartók's 'axis' system of harmony, keys in the same mode at the distance of a tritone are alternatives and may be interchanged without doing violence to harmonic logic. See Roy Howat, 'Bartok, Lendvai and the Principles of Proportional Analysis', in *Music Analysis*, 2/1, March 1983, 69–95.

[39] Copland's own technical term in general: see p. 124.

and with special emphasis the C sharps in the prolonged G major section from bar 48, the singer articulating this feature for the first time:

Ex. 5.4: 'Going to Heaven!', bars 48–53
© Copyright 1951 by the Aaron Copland Fund for Music, Inc., copyright renewed.
Boosey & Hawkes, Inc., sole licensee.

At the reprise, in the achingly exposed vocal solo that many might consider a climactic point of the composition, or one of its climactic points (this solo has been presaged to some extent by the music of Ex. 5.4 above), the tritone (E) appears in the tonic, at the actual pitch that is going to become the closing tonality of the song some moments later:

Ex. 5.5: 'Going to Heaven!', voice only, bars 91⁶–95
© Copyright 1951 by the Aaron Copland Fund for Music, Inc., copyright renewed.
Boosey & Hawkes, Inc., sole licensee.

If such correspondences between detail and structure are the stuff of modern Western classical music, as practitioners as well as theorists of recent centuries have tended to agree, it must nevertheless be counted as a particularly choice example when the composer seizes such a moment as a shaft of poetic substance in such a way as this:

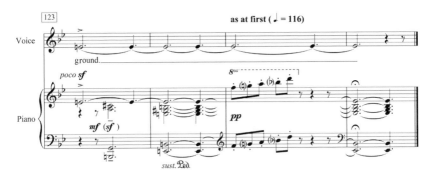

Ex. 5.6: 'Going to Heaven!', bars 123–6 (= last system)
© Copyright 1951 by the Aaron Copland Fund for Music, Inc., copyright renewed.
Boosey & Hawkes, Inc., sole licensee.

It was said above that this moment is 'as unexpected as it is poignant – and poetically decisive'. Four of the five notes of the 'Going to Heaven!' motive here are chromatic in E (F, G, B flat and D). Scales a tritone apart are inherently chromatically distinct and tend to form twelve-note aggregates, so perhaps we should not set too much store by the fact that in bars 124–5 Copland is using eleven of the possible twelve pitches (only C sharp is missing, after its sustained presence in the preceding twenty-one bars from bar 103). Still, there is no reason not to imagine his pleasure in having 'found' this idea, an archetypal Romantic reminiscence, yet a kind of memory imprinted here in the language of advanced harmony that would have been unthinkable, more or less, in Dickinson's times, rather like a photomontage perhaps, emblematic of the 'collage' world of the twentieth century,[40] and using means of expression that were not yet available in most of the nineteenth.

Linguistically only to be expected, then, strategically 'historically predictable' to use the earlier turn of phrase, as a compositional tactic at this point in the music the closing reminiscence nevertheless comes as a lightning strike – 'poignant' if you will – with a certain light-heartedness that emanates from the comfort of the familiar (this is now a well-entrenched

---

[40] Glenn Watkins, in *Pyramids at the Louvre: Music, Culture, and Collage from Stravinsky to the Postmodernists*, Cambridge, Mass., Harvard University Press, 1994, discusses this feature of his period extensively. See also Chapter 4, note 42.

motif, and B flat major has become the referential harmony). Let us recall Gustav Jenner from Chapter 2 pointing out (in 1905, remembering his studies with Brahms from 1888) that one must often wonder why, in what he then called 'modern' song, a composition necessarily had to end in the key in which it started (see pp. 50–1). Here is Copland providing a mid-twentieth-century answer that Jenner had not considered, or perhaps been in a position to consider, at the end of the nineteenth: that a structure may well be an organic tonal 'journey' but ending elsewhere than it began. The idea is poetically decisive in 'Going to Heaven!' because of the semantic, albeit wordless message; one might even call it a flashback. This, along with much else besides in Copland's song, is what one is entitled to call 'remarkable aesthetically', to return to the former point. The *device* of thematic recall, even as specifically defined as this case, did of course exist. Schumann's 'Kennst du das Land?' offers an example of an uncannily similar situation where his voice announces a distant place or '*Land*' (compared with Copland's distant universe or 'heaven') signalled by a melodic fragment that the piano brings back in a last valediction that goes, it might be said, and just as here in the Dickinson song, beyond words. Something akin to this also occurs in Schubert's 'First Loss', where, too, the piano takes on the melodic mantle of the voice to provide a last, nonverbal word (see Exs. 5.2 and 5.3). Yet only the transvocal resources of a new musical age were able to allow Copland to add in this way, musically, a sense of temporal multidimensionality to Dickinson's verbal construction, to add something that the reader might freely admit does make her words sing.

Not that they start to sing only at the end. Even Copland's first musical idea opens up a vast potential musicopoetic landscape. What is this long, loud, proud, grace-noted F telling us? It raps at the very door to heaven? While I do not make any specific connection with Kafka (see Chapter 4, pp. 88–9 in particular), the reader may enjoy contemplating whether Dickinson's spirited, heaven-bound persona would have behaved in the moribund way that we saw of Kafka's threshold-stuck man. It is a point worth considering if it reminds us of the gap – some would call it a gulf – between twentieth-century European existential anxiety with its appropriate gloominess and the frisky Americanism of the prescient, Romantic Dickinson and the nostalgic, 'modern' Copland; 'Americanism' that is, surely, every bit as momentous, and which may yet come to be thought of as actually more 'serious' in its vitality or piquancy than the angst of that colder ethos, not that anyone is giving prizes. The twenty-first-century singer (gloriously unaware of those historical musings) tries to attain length and height on the antidictional syllable '-ven' on Ds and then

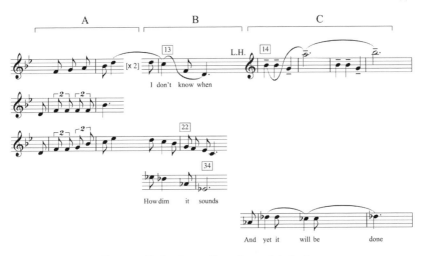

Ex. 5.7: Copland: paradigmatic vocal derivation
© Copyright 1951 by the Aaron Copland Fund for Music, Inc., copyright renewed.
Boosey & Hawkes, Inc., sole licensee.

up to F, extending over 2, 17 and then 20 quavers respectively (bars 3–6). It
will seem then as if any sustained pitch is going to ask us for interpretation,
ask to be understood: 'when' from bar 13, 'astonished' from bar 20 on
another antidictional syllable, '-sh[ed]', and so on swinging from high to
low long final notes, which the accompaniment adopts, too, for instance
with the rasping B (natural) introducing the 'you're going too . . .?' surprise
(see Ex. 5.4), and eventually the entire closing section with its long and
partly very deep, sustained chords in the accompaniment, orchestrated so
fetchingly in the 1970 version.

But it is not just 'ideas' at the musical surface that flood Copland's technique here. His composer's ear is working right to the roots of the musical
structure. Ex. 5.7 begins to reveal some of this, choosing on this occasion
an archaeological approach, digging down, which is after all less theatrical in terms of analytical exegesis than showing a simple generative model
arriving at a complex (and already known) musical surface – although these
approaches do in the end amount to the same phenomenon as hierarchical
models of the linear musical surface. Ex. 5.7 shows under paradigm 'C'
what might be called the third musical 'idea', in the piano (from bar 14).
It does not need a sophisticated argument to maintain that this piano line
amounts to, or elaborates, or prolongs, a 'neighbouring-note' figure, the
complete lower neighbouring-note figure for a B flat (B flat / A / B flat;

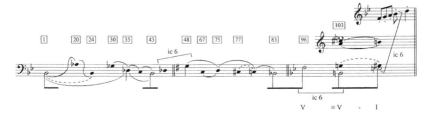

Ex. 5.8: Copland: graph.

slurred in this example). We can also see in Ex. 5.7 that taking the voice in paradigms 'A' and 'B', top system, together shows the vocal 'origin' of this in the notes D – C – D (slurred in this example). Then under paradigm C it is evident that these neighbouring-note figures 'generate' the new material in the voice, where the neighbouring-note figure is diatonic within the local harmony of G flat major, thus D flat / C flat / D flat (and not using the tritone, or sharpened, 'octatonic' fourth degree, C).

Ex. 5.8 shows by means of a bass-line graph, aiming to go to what was called above 'the roots of the musical structure', or at least some of the most important roots, that the lower neighbouring-note figure is the means of harmonic prolongation (B flat / A flat / B flat) of the entire first 29 bars. This mode of analysis has been continued right to the end of the song, giving a structural graph of the entire composition and inviting considerable comment, likely in the work of any commentator to focus on the following two points. Firstly, it is evident that the whole flow of the bulk of the song, up to the final reprise area (see bar 96) and to the subsequent swerve to the tritone E tonicized by its dominant harmony B, relies on a symmetrical prolongation around the main tonic B flat, through the upper flat mediant (D flat major from bar 35) and the submediant (G major from bar 48), harmonic regions four semitones above and below the tonic respectively. Secondly, although the first 'move' to D flat unfolds in ways that could easily be found in a Schubert song (see the bass-line graph for bars 1–35), the second move, D flat to the G at bar 48, and the third, F to the B at bar 103, are both tritonal (augmented fourth and diminished fifth respectively) and, for want of a better epithet, modernistic, at least in terms of the kind of long-gone major-minor 'grammar' that lies at the heart of traditional theories such as Schenker's. If we add to those comments the delicately subcutaneous stepwise progressions such as those from B flat (see bars 20 and 30) and from D, the dominant of G (see bars 75ff.), there is a complete 'reading' here; it is Copland's plot.

Those used to following musical plots in tonally oriented pieces will immediately take in from Ex. 5.8 the sense of journey, exciting but coherent, arriving at an unexpected place that one can nevertheless understand. One may take Dickinson entirely at face value with her 'I don't know when' about going to heaven, and feel that Copland, too, is not imposing events on the poem. It would be not only crass to say that B flat is earth and the eventual E is heaven, but also simply wrong, rather in the way that we have disparaged the idea of 'songfulness' as being suspect because of the much more complex assumptions on which it rests (see p. 5). Both the poem and its music are about potentialities, enforced musings: once you decide to step on to this ride, it will take you where it will; and so in understanding it there is a certain figuring-out needed, even an alienation about it all, a kind of mechanistic, clinical poietic underpinning that for many people is synonymous with the 'modern', and the emotional portent of which makes it of unquestionable artistic value, something not to be assimilated, as it were, 'only' casually. With those thoughts in mind, I invite the reader to revisit some of Paglia's words: 'the relation of form to content is aggressive and draconian . . . The brutality of this belle of Amherst would stop a truck.'[41] Whatever Copland's secret, personal thoughts may have been, that, it seems to me, is one way of characterizing his own raw creativity in response to Dickinson.

[41] See p. 124.

CHAPTER 6

By way of brief conclusion

At an early stage of this argument and exegesis I expressed dissatisfaction with Lawrence Kramer's idea of 'songfulness' (see p. 5), not because it is a bad idea, which would hardly be likely of such an imaginative and thoughtful critic, but because it is too complex. Kramer's 'just singing', as will have been inferred almost incidentally when examining *Stripsody* (see pp. 107–14), is an idealized, formulaic, reductionist comforter of a thought, not a serious proposition susceptible to extrapolation through an evidence-based study of actual songs. Kramer's desire to demystify vocality by restoring it out of the clutches of arcane, positivist scholarly dissection to the pure and simple experience of genius at work is as laudable now as its more authoritative version was more than two millennia ago, when Plato asked us to realize that we perceive through the eye of the mind, as he would have it, and not through the highways and byways of sophisticated verbal reasoning and rhetoric; perception, in its simplest form, is a matter of immediate recognition, not of forensic analysis. But signification does not come in convenient packets. What we hear in a performance of a song is also what we brought to that performance from our experience, what we remember of it, and what it will become. This is actually the most obvious single challenge to music analysis, and even more of a challenge to that very poor relation of analysis, music criticism: how do you know what you will say about a piece of music *tomorrow*? It does not mean that one must throw in the towel and give up entirely on having the confidence to say anything at all about music, but it does mean that one ought to have good reason and good evidence.

There is, in this author's view at least, no good *reason* to celebrate 'songfulness' as an inaccessible, inscrutable, mysterious quality about which nothing worthwhile can be observed, learnt, handed on. If one cannot ask the question 'what is it that allows words to be intoned in a certain way that is categorically different from speech yet comprehensible?', we are never going to understand much about a kind of art that everyone, everywhere, regards as sublime (by which I mean look at world musics and popular music and their historical equivalents over thousands of years of human evolution and ask what form virtually all of it takes and took). It is, then, with good reason that the attempt has been made here to look into the magical interior spaces of music and words, avoiding the laissez-faire factual accumulation of 'New Musicology' at its most 'correct', while equally avoiding the tendency of the least worthwhile kinds of music analysis merely to describe the known rather than to explain what was not previously known.

As to what is good evidence, this is part and parcel of the same line of argument, while bringing in aesthetic issues that I do not claim to have solved, but only to have tried to remain aware of, consistently. What counts as 'evidence' in discussing musical substance depends on what we decide is referring to what. Naomi Cumming, a brilliant philosopher of music, put this in a particularly striking way, striking because of her customary clarity and also because of what follows from her thoughts:

> Consider again descriptions such as those made by the critics of violin performances, where terms for 'voice' or 'singing', modified in various ways, are quite common. These descriptions give a signifying capacity to violinistic sounds comparable to that of expressive tones of voice . . . There is, however, no physically distinct 'object' to which the sound refers. When you hear 'singing' in the violin's sound, the singing is *in* the sound, not somewhere else. On hearing the sounds, you hear certain properties of singing as belonging to them, whether or not you articulate that thought or make it explicit. 'Singing' is not, then, an object to which you imagine they refer (although you might be reminded of an operatic singer), but a quality that seems to be presented in the sounds. Thoughts of 'singing' or 'vocality', as typically experienced in Western traditions of performance, may certainly inform listening, but they do not need to become the explicit objects of thought as you are attending to these sounds. Suppose that a particular quality of 'voice' attracts your attention, one that is not captured precisely by another performer, or perhaps even by the same performer at another time (or in a different acoustic environment). A recognition of its individual quality implies that some comparison has informed your listening. That comparison can, however, remain entirely tacit until a moment of critical reflection, when it becomes more articulate.[1]

This states precisely, in one way, a recurrent aesthetic premise of the 'evidence' that has been adduced here from Schubert and Schoenberg, Brahms, Copland and the rest, and by implication from all modern Western song ranging from the fine to the miraculous (how *that* distinction can be determined I do not venture to say). I would only ask, and not in the least

---

[1] Naomi Cumming, *The Sonic Self: Musical Subjectivity and Signification*, Bloomington, Indiana University Press, 2000, 73–4.

by way of criticism since I find the arguments in Cumming's magnificent study to be on all fours from cover to cover, to what, if to anything, vocality itself refers? You hear certain 'properties of singing' in singing, too. Every great voice has that 'particular quality of "voice"' that is its voice. What is more, this is in the ear – I am absolutely sure – of each composer we study. Whether or not Brahms 'heard' in his inner ear a particular singer singing 'Von ewiger Liebe' or an ideal singer or the sum or (as it may better be expressed) the essence of his experiences of vocality, we just cannot know. It would be counterintuitive, however, and a waste of our time and attention, to wonder whether Brahms had some species of *abstract*, disembodied, virtual 'Von ewiger Liebe' in mind, any more than we would be right to imagine Schoenberg puzzling out 'merely' contrapuntal solutions in *Friede auf Erden* rather than dreaming his wondrous choral soundscapes, or Berberian allowing that any old approximate sight-reading stomp through *Stripsody* would do rather than the exquisitely nuanced vocal choreography to be heard in her recording.

There may even be a hint of priority lurking in Cumming's disquisition, which would be likely to emerge if one were to speculate, troping her words: suppose that a particular quality of the *violinistic* 'attracts your attention' in a particular *song*. It seems to be an unlikely scenario. I defer to nobody in my adoration of the violin, and it has never been an intention in this book to imply or even hint in the least that instrumental music is in any rational or experiential or any other sense less important or meaningful, and so on, than vocal music. It has, however, been a persistent intention to put next to Peter Kivy's question (see Chapter 1, pp. 14–15, and it is one of the leitmotives in his extensive writings) – that is, next to the question of what we think we mean by absolute music and why people fail to comprehend the magnitude of what is being asked – *the* comparator question, implied by the title of this book, referred to recurrently within it, and not likely to be answered. Actually it has not once been asked, explicitly, what makes words sing; I hope the reader will be as content as the author with the participle, 'making', whoever is doing it.

Bibliography

Abbate, Carolyn, *Unsung Voices: Opera and Musical Narrative in the Nineteenth Century*, Princeton, Princeton University Press, 1991

In Search of Opera, Princeton, Princeton University Press, 2001

Adorno, Theodor W., 'Schubert', in *Gesammelte Schriften*, vol. xvii, Frankfurt, Suhrkamp, 1997, 18–33

Agawu, Kofi, 'Analyzing Music under the New Musicological Regime', in *Music Theory On-Line*, 2/4, May 1996

Austin, William, 'Words and Music: Theory and Practice of 20th-Century Composers', in *Words and Music: The Composer's View*, ed. Lawrence Berman, Cambridge, Mass., Harvard University Press, 1971, 1–8

Ayrey, Craig, 'Berg's "Scheideweg": Analytical Issues in Op. 2/ii', in *Music Analysis*, 1/2, July 1982, 189–202

Bailey, Kathryn, *The Twelve-Note Music of Anton Webern*, Cambridge, Cambridge University Press, 1991

Banks, Paul, 'Fin-de-siècle Vienna: Politics and Modernism', in *Man & Music: The Late Romantic Era from the Mid-19th Century to World War I*, ed. Jim Samson, London, Macmillan, 1991, 362–88

Bannan, Nicholas, 'The Role of the Voice in Human Development', PhD dissertation, University of Reading, 2002

Barazzom, Beatrice, 'Kurtág's Music: The Spectacle of Nature, the Breath of History – from Opp. 7 to 27', in *Studia Musicologica*, 143/3–4, 2002, 253–67

Barthes, Roland, *Writing Degree Zero*, New York, Hill and Wang, 1968

S/Z, New York, Hill and Wang, 1974

Baudelaire, Charles, *The Painter of Modern Life and Other Essays*, London, Phaidon, 1964

Beckett, Samuel, *Poems in English by Samuel Beckett*, New York, Grove Press, 1961

Beckles Willson, Rachel, 'An Analytical Study of György Kurtág's *The Sayings of Péter Boremisza*, Opus 7 (1963–68)', PhD dissertation, King's College, London, 1998

'Bulgarian Rhythm and its Disembodiment in *The Sayings of Péter Bornemisza*, Op. 7, in *Studia Musicologica*, 43/3–4, 2002, 269–80

Bell, A. Craig, *Brahms, The Vocal Music*, London, Associated University Presses, 1996

Bennett, Paula, *Emily Dickinson: Woman Poet*, Hemel Hempstead, Harvester Wheatsheaf, 1990

Bent, Ian (ed.), *Music Theory in the Age of Romanticism*, Cambridge, Cambridge University Press, 1996

Berg, Alban, 'Why is Schoenberg's Music So Hard to Understand?', in *Contemporary Composers on Contemporary Music*, ed. E. Schwartz and B. Childs, New York, Da Capo Press, 1967, 59–71.

Bernstein, Leonard, *The Unanswered Question: Six Talks at Harvard*, Cambridge, Mass., Harvard University Press, 1976

Biedermann, Hans, *Knaurs Lexikon der Symbole*, Munich, Droemer Knaur, 1989

Bloom, Harold, *The Anxiety of Influence: A Theory of Poetry*, New York, Oxford University Press, 1973

Boss, Jack, 'Schoenberg's Op. 22 Radio Talk and Developing Variation in Atonal Music', in *Music Theory Spectrum*, 14/2, Fall 1992, 125–49

Brăiloiu, Constantin, *Problems of Ethnomusicology*, Cambridge, Cambridge University Press, 1984

Bujic, Bojan, *Music in European Thought 1851–1912*, Cambridge, Cambridge University Press, 1988

Burnham, Scott, 'The Second Nature of Sonata Form', in Clark and Rehding 2001, 111–41

Butler, Christopher, *Interpretation, Deconstruction, and Ideology: An Introduction to Some Current Issues in Literary Theory*, Oxford, Clarendon Press, 1984

Cahn, Steven, 'Variations in Manifold Time: Historical Consciousness in the Music and Writings of Arnold Schoenberg', PhD dissertation, State University of New York, Stony Brook, 1996

Christensen, Thomas, 'Music Theory and Its Histories', in *Music Theory and the Exploration of the Past*, ed. Christopher Hatch and David Berstein, Chicago, University of Chicago Press, 1993, 1–39

Christensen, Thomas (ed.), *The Cambridge History of Western Music Theory*, Cambridge, Cambridge University Press, 2002

Chua, Daniel, 'Vincenzo Galilei, Modernity and the Division of Nature', in Clark and Rehding 2001, 17–29

Clark, Suzannah, and Rehding, Alexander, *Music Theory and Natural Order from the Renaissance to the Early Twentieth Century*, Cambridge, Cambridge University Press, 2001

Cody, John, *After Great Pain: The Inner Life of Emily Dickinson*, Cambridge, Mass., Harvard University Press, 1971

Colles, Henry, *Brahms*, London, The Bodley Head, 1920

Cone, Edward, 'Poet's Love or Composer's Love?', in *Music and Text: Critical Inquiries*, ed. Stephen Scher, Cambridge, Cambridge University Press, 1992, 177–92

Cook, Nicholas, *A Guide to Musical Analysis*, London, Dent, 1987

　Music, Imagination, and Culture, Oxford, Clarendon Press, 1990

Copland, Aaron, *Music and Imagination*, Cambridge, Mass., Harvard University Press, 1952

Copland, Aaron, and Perlis, Vivian, *Copland Since 1943*, New York, St Martin's Press, 1989

Culler, Jonathan, *Structuralist Poetics: Structuralism, Linguistics and the Study of Literature*, Ithaca, Cornell University Press, 1975

    Literary Theory: A Very Short Introduction, Oxford, Oxford University Press, 1997

Cumming, Naomi, *The Sonic Self: Musical Subjectivity and Signification*, Bloomington, Indiana University Press, 2000

Dahlhaus, Carl, *Between Romanticism and Modernism*, Berkeley, University of California Press, 1980

Damasio, Antonio, *The Feeling of What Happens: Body, Emotion and the Making of Consciousness*, London, Vintage, 2000

Danuser, Hermann, 'Lyrik und Weltanschauungsmusik beim frühen Schönberg: Bemerkungen zu Opus 4 und Opus 13', in *Arnold Schönberg – Neuerer der Musik*, ed. Rudolf Stefan and Sigrid Wiesmann, Vienna, Lafite, 1996, 24–31

Darwin, Charles, *The Expression of the Emotions in Man and Animals*, London, John Murray, 1904, 2nd ed.

de la Motte, Diether, *Musikalische Analyse, mit kritischen Anmerkungen von Carl Dahlhaus*, Cassel, Bärenreiter, 1968

Derrida, Jacques, *Spurs: Nietzsche's Styles*, Chicago, University of Chicago Press, 1979

Dickinson, Emily, *Emily Dickinson: The Complete Poems*, ed. T. Johnson, London, Faber, 1975

Donat, Misha, '4 Gesänge, Opus 43', in *The Compleat Brahms: A Guide to the Musical Works of Johannes Brahms*, ed. Leon Botstein, New York, Norton, 1999, 229–34

Dunsby, Jonathan, 'Schoenberg's Premonition, Op. 22, No. 4, in Retrospect', in *Journal of the Arnold Schoenberg Institute*, 1/3, 1977, 137–49

    '*Pierrot Lunaire* and the Resistance to Theory', in *The Musical Times*, 130, 1989, 732–6

    Schoenberg: Pierrot lunaire, Cambridge, Cambridge University Press, 1992

    'Recent Schenker: The Poetic Power of Intelligent Calculation (or, The Emperor's Second Set of New Clothes)', in *Music Analysis*, 18/2, July 1999, 263–73

    'Chamber Music and Piano', in Samson 2002, 500–21

    'Friede auf Erden Op. 13', in *Arnold Schönberg: Interpretationen seiner Werke*, ed. Gerold Gruber, Laaber, Laaber-Verlag, 2002, 172–80

    'Thematic and Motivic Analysis', in *The Cambridge History of Music Theory*, ed. Thomas Christensen, Cambridge, Cambridge University Press, 2002, 907–26

    'All the Dancers know it and it is Valid for All Times: Goehr, Kafka and The Law of the Quadrille', in *Sing, Ariel: Essays and Thoughts for Alexander Goehr's Seventieth Birthday*, ed. Alison Latham, Aldershot, Ashgate, 2003, 171–9

Dunsby, Jonathan, and Whittall, Arnold, *Music Analysis in Theory and Practice*, London, Faber, 1988

Eberwein, Jane Donahue, *Dickinson: Strategies of Limitation*, Amherst, University of Massachusetts Press, 1985

Ernst, Katharina, *'Death' in the Poetry of Emily Dickinson*, Heidelberg, Carl Winter Universitätsverlag, 1992

Evans, Edwin, *Historical, Descriptive, & Analytical Account of the Entire Works of Johannes Brahms: The Vocal Works*, London, Reeves, 1912

Ferlazzo, Paul, *Emily Dickinson*, Boston, Twayne, 1976

Fink, Robert, 'Going Flat: Post-Hierarchical Music Theory and the Musical Surface', in *Rethinking Music*, ed. Nicholas Cook and Mark Everist, Oxford, Oxford University Press, 1999, 102–37

Georgiades, Thrasybulos, *Music and Language: The Rise of Western Music as Exemplified in Settings of the Mass*, Cambridge, Cambridge University Press, 1982

Goehr, Alexander, *Finding the Key: Selected Writings of Alexander Goehr*, ed. Derrick Puffett, London, Faber, 1998

'What's Left to be Done?', *The Musical Times*, 140, Summer 1999, 19–28

Goehr, Lydia, *The Quest for Voice: On Music, Politics, and the Limits of Philosophy*, Oxford, Clarendon Press, 1998

Guthrie, James, *Emily Dickinson's Vision: Illness and Identity in Her Poetry*, Gainesville, University Press of Florida, 1998

Habermas, Jürgen, *Knowledge and Human Interests*, Oxford, Polity Press, 1987

Hagenbüchte, Roland, 'Dickinson and Literary Theory', in G. Grabher et al., *The Emily Dickinson Handbook*, Amherst, University of Massachusetts Press, 1998, 356–84

Halász, Péter, *György Kurtág*, Budapest, Magus, 1998

Hanslick, Eduard, *On the Musically Beautiful*, Indianapolis, Hackett Publishing Company, 1986

Harrison, Max, *The Lieder of Brahms*, London, Cassell, 1972

Heller, F. C. (ed.), *Arnold Schönberg, Franz Schreker Briefwechsel mit unveröff. Texten von Arnold Schönberg*, Tützing, Schneider, 1974

Howat, Roy, 'Bartok, Lendvai and the Principles of Proportional Analysis', in *Music Analysis*, 2/1, March 1983, 69–95

Ivey, Donald, 'The Romantic Synthesis in Selected Settings of Goethe's "Kennst du das Land?" ', DMA dissertation, University of Illinois at Urbana-Champaign, 1962

Jameux, Dominique, *L'Ecole de Vienne*, Paris, Fayard, 2002

Jenner, Gustav, 'Brahms as Man, Teacher, and Artist', in *Brahms and His World*, ed. Walter Frisch, Princeton, Princeton University Press, 1990, 185–204

Johnson, Julian, *Who Needs Classical Music?*, Oxford, Oxford University Press, 2002

Jones, Steve, *Almost Like a Whale:* The Origin of Species *Updated*, London, Doubleday, 1999

Jost, Christa, *Mendelssohns Lieder ohne Worte*, Tützing, Schneider, 1988

Kafka, Franz, *The Collected Short Stories of Franz Kafka*, Harmondsworth, Penguin, 1988

Kalbeck, Max, *Johannes Brahms*, Berlin, Deutsche Brahms-Gesellschaft, 1921, 3rd ed.

Kandinsky, Wassily, 'On the Question of Form', in *The 'Blaue Reiter' Almanac*, ed. Wassily Kandinsky and Franz Marc, New York, Viking Press, 1974, 147–87

Keller, Hans, *Criticism*, London, Faber, 1987

Keller, K., *The Only Kangaroo Among the Beauty: Emily Dickinson and America*, Baltimore, Johns Hopkins University Press, 1979

Kerman, Joseph, 'How We Got into Analysis, and How to Get Out', *Critical Inquiry*, 7, 1980, 311–31

Musicology, London, Fontana, 1985

Kivy, Peter, *The Fine Art of Repetition: Essays in the Philosophy of Music*, Cambridge, Cambridge University Press, 1993

Kramer, Lawrence, *Music and Poetry: The Nineteenth Century and After*, Berkeley, University of California Press, 1984

'Performance and Social Meaning in the Lied: Schubert's Erster Verlust', in *Current Musicology*, 56, 1994, 5–23

Classical Music and Postmodern Knowledge, Berkeley, University of California Press, 1995

Franz Schubert: Sexuality, Subjectivity, Song, Cambridge, Cambridge University Press, 1998

Musical Meaning: Toward a Critical History, Berkeley, University of California Press, 2002

Kraus, Karl, *Half-Truths and One-and-a-Half Truths*, ed. H. Zohn, Manchester, Carcanet, 1986

Krones, Hartmut, 'Arnold Schönberg: Friede auf Erden, Op. 13', in *Österreichische Musikzeitschrift*, 53/3–4, 1988, 55–7

Kuna, Franz, 'The Janus-faced Novel: Conrad, Musil, Kafka, Mann', in *Modernism 1890–1930*, ed. Malcolm Bradbury and James McFarlane, Harmondsworth, Penguin Books, 1991, 443–52

Meyer, Leonard, *Emotion and Meaning in Music*, Chicago, University of Chicago Press, 1956

Miller, Cristanne, *Emily Dickinson: A Poet's Grammar*, Cambridge, Mass., Harvard University Press, 1987

Mitchell, Domhnall, *Emily Dickinson: Monarch of Perception*, Amherst, University of Massachusetts Press, 2000

Mithen, Steven, *The Prehistory of the Mind: A Search for the Origins of Art, Religion and Science*, London, Thames and Hudson, 1996

Nattiez, Jean-Jacques, *Music and Discourse: Toward a Semiology of Music*, Princeton, Princeton University Press, 1990

(ed.), *The Boulez–Cage Correspondence*, Cambridge, Cambridge University Press, 1993

Wagner Androgyne: A Study in Interpretation, Princeton, Princeton University Press, 1993

The Battle of Chronos and Orpheus, Oxford, Oxford University Press, 2004

Newbould, Brian, *Schubert: The Music and the Man*, London, Gollancz, 1997

Paglia, Camille, *Sexual Personae: Art and Decadence from Nefertiti to Emily Dickinson*, New Haven, Yale University Press, 1990

Perrey, Beate, *Schumann's Dichterliebe and Early Romantic Poetics: Fragmentation of Desire*, Cambridge, Cambridge University Press, 2002

Phillips, Adam, *On Kissing, Tickling and Being Bored*, London, Faber, 1993

Darwin's Worms, London, Faber, 1999

Houdini's Box: On the Arts of Escape, London, Faber, 2001

Pollack, Howard, *Aaron Copland: The Life and Work of an Uncommon Man*, London, Faber, 2000

Reed, John, *Schubert (The Master Musicians)*, London, Dent, 1987

Reich, Nancy, 'Fanny Hensel: The Power of Class', in *Mendelssohn and His World*, ed. R. Larry Todd, Princeton, Princeton University Press, 1991, 86–99

Reich, Willi, *Schoenberg: A Critical Biography*, Harlow, Longman, 1971

Rosen, Charles, *The Romantic Generation*, London, HarperCollins, 1996

Ruf, Wolfgang, '*Vier Lieder für Gesang und Orchester*, Op. 22', in *Arnold Schönberg: Interpretationen seiner Werke*, ed. Gerold Gruber, Laaber, Laaber-Verlag, 2002, 1, 321–32

Sams, Eric, ' "Von ewiger Liebe" ', in *Neue Zeitschrift für Musik*, 133, 257

Samson, Jim (ed.), *The Cambridge History of Nineteenth-Century Music*, Cambridge, Cambridge University Press, 2002

Schmalfeldt, Janet, 'Berg's Path to Atonality', in *Alban Berg: Historical and Analytical Perspectives*, ed. D. Gable and R. Morgan, Oxford, Clarendon, 1990, 79–109

Schmidt, Christian Martin, 'Zukunftsverheissung und musikalische Zielgerichtetheit: Arnold Schönbergs Chor Friede auf Erden Op. 13', in *Berliner Beiträge zur Mussikwissenschaft: Beihefte zur Neuen Berlinischen Musikzeitung*, 9/1, 1994, 40–5

Schoenberg, Arnold, 'Analysis of the Four Orchestral Songs Opus 22', in *Perspectives of New Music*, 3/2, Spring-Summer 1965, 1–21

Fundamentals of Musical Composition, London, Faber, 1970

Preliminary Exercises in Counterpoint, London 1970, 2nd ed.

Berliner Tagebuch, Frankfurt am Main, Propyläen Verlag, 1974

Style and Idea: Selected Writing of Arnold Schoenberg, London, Faber, 1975

'The Relationship to the Text', in Schoenberg 1975, 141–5

'Why New Melodies are Difficult to Understand', in Bryan Simms, 'New Documents in the Schoenberg-Schenker Polemic', in *Perspectives of New Music*, 16/1, 1977, 115–6

The Musical Idea and the Logic, Technique, and Art of its Presentation, ed. and trans. Patricia Carpenter and Severine Neff, New York, Columbia University Press, 1993

Shreffler, Anne, ' "Mein Weg geht jetzt vorüber": The Vocal Origins of Webern's Twelve-Note Composition', in *Journal of the American Musicological Society*, 47, 1994, 275–339

Sick, Thomas, ' "Unsere Liebe muss ewig bestehn!": Liebestreue in Brahms' Lied-schaffen', in *Brahms als Liedkomponist: Studien zum Verhältnis von Text und Vertonung*, ed. Peter Jost, Stuttgart, F. Steiner, 1992, 173–89

Simms, Bryan, *The Atonal Music of Arnold Schoenberg, 1908–1923*, Oxford, Oxford University Press, 2000

Sylvester, David, *About Modern Art: Critical Essays 1948–97*, London, Pimlico, 1997

Taruskin, Richard, 'The Presence of the Past and the Pastness of the Present', in *Text and Act: Essays on Music and Performance*, Oxford, Oxford University Press, 1995, 90–154

Thwaite, Anthony (ed.), *Philip Larkin: Collected Poems*, London, Faber, 1988

Walsh, Stephen, 'György Kurtág: An Outline Study (I)', in *Tempo*, 140, March 1982, 11–21

Watkins, Glenn, *Pyramids at the Louvre: Music, Culture, and Collage from Stravinsky to the Postmodernists*, Cambridge, Mass., Harvard University Press, 1994

Webern, Anton von, 'Schönbergs Musik', in [no author], *Arnold Schönberg mit Beiträgen von Alban Berg, Paris von Gütersloh, K. Horwitz, Heinrich Jalowetz, W. Kandinsky, Paul Königer, Karl Linke, Robert Neumann, Erwin Stein, Ant. v. Webern, Egon Wellesz*, publisher unknown, Munich 1912, 22–4

Whittall, Arnold, *Musical Composition in the Twentieth Century*, Oxford, Oxford University Press, 1999

Exploring Twentieth-Century Music: Tradition and Innovation, Cambridge, Cambridge University Press, 2003

Wintle, Christopher, 'Webern's Lyric Character', in *Webern Studies*, ed. Kathryn Bailey, Cambridge, Cambridge University Press, 1996, 229–63.

Zuckerkandl, Victor, *Man the Musician: Sound and Symbol, Volume Two*, Princeton, Princeton University Press, 1976

Index